Gourmet Camping Cuisine

Menus for rafting, canoeing, camping, and RVers

Marilynn Murphey Machin

ISBN-10: 0-9771694-0-5
ISBN-13: 978-0-9771694-0-5

First Edition

Cartoon illustrations by Marilynn Murphey Machin.
Photographs by Marilynn Murphey Machin, except as noted.
Front cover: Selway River, ID.
Back cover: Escalante River, UT and Usumacinta River, Mexico by James Machin.
Layout by Dave Winkler.
Printed in U.S.A.

For ordering and distribution information contact:

Marilynn Murphey Machin
8409 Bell Mountain Drive
Austin, TX 78730
mmmbooks@sbcglobal.net
www.rivermaps.net/mmmbooks

mmm…books!

Bon Apetit!
Dinner, Page 187

Table of Contents

Dedication

Acknowledgments

Introduction

Tips

Abbreviations

DO....Dutch Oven
ZLB....Zip Loc Bag
MSB....Micro Seal Bag

Dedication

For my husband and best friend, James.

For my dear Mom, Frances E. Murphey who taught me to cook and to appreciate and respect nature. And in loving memory of my Dad, Robert E. Murphey, who introduced me to camping and taught me that life is an adventure to be experienced throughout my lifetime. To my sweet sisters and brothers, Jennifer, Patty, Becky, Barbara, Robert, Marjorie, Dan, and Kathryn. I have many fond memories of our camping trips and childhood years together.

To all my canoeing and rafting friends, you know who you are, and everyone that has ever enjoyed being outdoors. See y'all on the river or in camp.

Acknowledgments

I wish to thank my husband, James, for his encouragement, never ending patience, and editing.

Peter Ryan, wherever you are these days. Thank you for planting the "seed" in writing this book and helping to make our first trip down the Grand Canyon an incredible and unforgettable experience.

To Sierra Mac River Trips in Groveland, California. Especially Marty McDonnell, Chris Condon, and Chef Armando Dominguez. I believe they were the first rafting company to have gourmet trips. They set the bar high at the very beginning. They also pioneered rafting down the beautiful Tuolumne river. If you have never done a trip with them you are missing out on a trip of a lifetime. Go do it. Thanks for your inspiration and friendship through the years.

For George Gardiner, one of the most talented artists I have the privilege to know, who used to work for Walt Disney. He taught me much of what I know about cartooning.

Introduction

Be sure to read the "Tips" following this introduction. There are important things here that are essential to making your recipe preparation easier.

It does not matter whether you are an expert or novice boater, camper, or RVer: we all like to eat well on our outdoor trips. This book was developed with rafting or canoeing trips in mind, but is suitable for any outdoor trip or in your own home. I want to encourage you to do your own river trip. Being a professional is not a requirement, but do you want to do it like the pros? Read on.

Unlike other cookbooks, this book is not a simple listing of recipes. It has fully planned out menus. This includes multiple, complete breakfast, lunch, and dinner menus for trips of up to 18 days. It will give you step by step instructions on what to do at home and on your trip for each menu. I've tried to add lots of variety to my menus so that you don't eat the same thing over and over. These are more on the gourmet side for people who like to eat well. If you want hardtack, tuna glop, and beanie weenies, you're out of luck.

In this book I have tried to make it easy for those of you who work and do not have time to organize or plan menus. This will show you how to prepare everything for a feast on the river. After all, it is hard to juggle family, work, and outdoor vacations. Who wants to get out in the middle of nowheresville and find out you left the sauce home for your great enchilada dinner - not I. You would have everyone on your back like maggots on dead meat. Or take the person who forgot to bring their meal - did they ever catch heat and I do not mean from a Coleman stove.

I kept hearing boaters, private and commercial, complaining about not having a planned-out and how-to cookbook, especially for novices and people who wanted good food but had little time to plan it. This book not only has incredible food but is also a time saver and helper.

My husband and I have been avid canoeists and rafters for decades. Food has always been an important part of our trips. I grew up in a family of nine children where many events centered around good home cooking.

Delicious, well planned and prepared food seems always to bring out a festive mood in people, especially on river trips. And it also allows more time for hiking, reading, or just laying around camp enjoying the company of your friends or the scenery.

This book is by no means the only way of doing something. It is intended to be a guide for those who enjoy being outdoors, and hopefully to make your trip more pleasurable.

These menus and recipes are a culmination of many incredible years on and off the river. So take a peek inside and float your way down a river into paradise.

I welcome any comments. Contact me at mmmbooks@sbcglobal.net.

Tips

- *Start coals for Dutch ovens (DOs) as first thing before preparing meal.*

- *Grilling: The grate should be 4 to 6 inches above the coals. Hardwood charcoal such as B&B Oak Lump Charcoal or Western Mesquite or Hickory Cookin Chunks are good to use in grilling b e c a u s e hardwood charcoal burns hotter, cleaner, and longer than charcoal briquettes and does a great job of searing in the natural flavors of meat. Although not necessary, you can place small amounts of soaked wood chips or fresh herbs on the coals to impart more flavors into the grilled food. Be careful, adding too many wood chips will cool your coals.*

Direct vs. Indirect Heat. Most grilling is done directly over the heat, but poultry tends to do better with indirect heat-with the coals on one side of the grill and the poultry on the other. It's a good idea to place the coals to the side anyway, so you'll have a "hot side" of the grill. Move food to the cooler area if there are flare-ups or if the food is cooking too quickly.

When are the coals ready? When the coals are bright red and still flaming, they're still too hot for most grilling. When the coals are red but covered with a light ash, the fire is hot. When they are covered in a thick ash, the fire is medium hot. Although it is not scientific, there is the "hand test" which can help you to determine a grill's heat. If you can hold your hand a couple of inches above the grate for less than a second, it's very hot, over 600 degrees. If you can hold it there three to four seconds, it's a medium heat, between 400 and 500 degrees. If you can hold your hand there for more than five seconds, you're feeling medium-low heat, in the range of 325 to 350 degrees. This is probably more than you ever wanted to know about grilling, but this is for all those engineers out there scratching their heads.

Powdered milk and/or eggs can be used instead of fresh. In recipes, they can generally be mixed with other dry ingredients and placed in Zip-Loc® bags (ZLB) before the trip. Add appropriate amount of additional water on the trip. Nonfat milk is widely available. Whole, spray-dried milk and powdered eggs are available at backpacking stores. Sterile milk, which can be stored warm, is also available.

Break fresh eggs carefully into wide-mouth plastic bottle (e.g. Nalgene®), before the trip. 5-6 large whole eggs equal 1 cup. The yolks will normally not break during the trip. You can freeze them in the bottle if you want them to last a little longer. If space allows you can also store eggs in styrofoam cartons in your cooler.

- *Egg Beaters is another alternative. They are a good substitute in recipes for whole, uncooked eggs. You are not supposed to freeze them and they recommend using within 7 days after opening.*

- *Place things in plastic bags, such as Zip-Loc®, Micro-Seal®, or Seal-A-Meal® (referred to in the recipes generically as ZLBs or MSBs), before the trip to save space and to get rid of excess packaging. MSB's are sealed shut by melting the top of the bag, and are generally stronger and more secure. Items to be frozen or that contain liquid should be either sealed in MSB's or double-bagged in the heavy-duty freezer ZLB's. Be sure to label the bags with the contents and which meal it is for.*

- *Pack your coolers as tightly as possible to minimize void space. Pack them in order of day(s) of use and label them. Coolers for later on will require more ice than earlier coolers. Place a layer of poly-fill insulation (buy at fabric shop) in the top of the cooler completely covering everything for extra insulation. After closing, run duct tape all around the joint between the lid and base. Bring a large beach towel* or bath mat to place over the cooler and then run a strap around the cooler to secure the lid. The towel can be doused with river water regularly to keep it wet and add evaporative cooling. Another idea is to get that foam-backed mylar sheet that is used for a windshield sun screen (buy at auto parts or discount store) or a space blanket and cover the cooler to reflect solar radiation.

Block ice lasts much longer than crushed. Do not buy supermarket fake block ice which has been made by compressing crushed ice into a block, because they do not last as long. Be sure you get solid blocks.

- For longer trips, have at least one cooler be ice only, and use it to re-ice food coolers. If you want your ice to last a little longer, put some dry ice in with the ice blocks. It's more expensive and may not be worth it to you.

- You can have one cooler be for frozen food only. Transfer frozen items into the fresh food cooler a day or two in advance to act as ice and to let it thaw.

- Pack dry food into waterproof "rocket boxes" or other dry boxes. As with coolers, pack them in order of days of use and label. Cans and other items with removable labels should be labeled with a waterproof marker in case the labels get wet and come off. You can even remove the labels in advance to minimize trash.

- We always have each person bring at least one surprise on our trips. It adds a lot of fun, and you never know when someone is going to pop out with one. It can be drink, food, costume, skit, dramatic reading, game, puzzle, instructional demonstration, musical instrument, art, handmade items, nebbishes, or anything else. Use your imagination.

Cheese: Hard block cheeses last longer than soft ones. Examples are cheddar, jack, parmesan, pecorino, manchego, emmental, and aged gruyere. Hard cheeses will freeze but may become crumbly when thawed. If this happens, use in cooking.

Bread: Buy bread with preservatives. It is also good to buy double wrapped breads like Pepperidge Farm or Oroweat because they will last longer. Rye bread also lasts longer. Store in dry boxes if possible. If any condensation forms inside the package, open it to allow it to dry out, or it will mold quickly. Refrigerator breads, the kind that pop open, are great baked in a DO but must be kept in a cooler. Canned bread, like Boston brown bread, is also good and can be stored anywhere.

Vegetables: Potatoes and onions can be stored in a small dry bag or a wooden or plastic ventilated crate strapped to your raft. They need to be able to air out if they get wet. Most other vegetables should be kept in a dry box or cooler. Store vegetables whole and unwashed whenever possible because they last longer. If using lettuce the first week of your trip, wash and dry it at home, layer it with paper towels to absorb moisture and put in a ZLB, press out air and store in cooler. This can be done with most all vegetables.

Fruit: Oranges, apples, melons, grapefruits, and whole pineapples are examples of the longest lasting fruits, and can be stored in a crate as with some of the vegetables. Usually any fruit with a somewhat harder exterior will last longer than fruit that has a softer exterior such as berries, bananas, pears, plums, and mangos. It is always best to buy fruit the day before a trip if possible.

Wines: It is best not to take glass on the river unless you have a well padded "rocket box" to store them in. Decant wine into cleaned plastic PET water or club soda bottles immediately before the trip. Squeeze to eliminate any head space and seal tightly. Four bottles of wine will fit in a 3 liter bottle, and five bottles will fit into a 1 gallon bottle. Don't use bottles from strongly flavored drinks or your wine may have an odd taste. Can you imagine what root beer wine would taste like on your trip?

Bacon can be purchased fully cooked and then reheated. It doesn't need refrigeration. I've tried this and it is actually good.

Drinks: Anything goes here. My husband even brews his own beer on the Grand Canyon. I'm surprised at how good it turns out. To keep drinks cold we use drag bags tied to the bow of our raft. Plastic gunny sacks (rice or feed bags) with rope threaded around the opening are very durable and cheap. It also helps hold the bow down in big rapids. For breakfast: orange juice, coffee, hot cocoa, hot tea. You need a good system for filtering your water.

• I always make recipes at home first. This helps to make my meals go smoother on the trip. And you can always make extra and freeze it. Just remember any recipe you make at home can be made on a river or camping trip.

Menu One

Days 1 - 4

Breakfast

Stuffed French Toast with Maple Syrup

Cantaloupe with Strawberries or Fruit in Season

Yogurt

Lunch

Vegetable-Cheese Stuffed Pita

Fresh Fruit in Season

Pickles and Peppers

Pepperidge Farm Cookies

Dinner

Fancy Nuts

Grilled Halibut or Salmon Steaks with Pesto Butter

Parsleyed Rice

Zucchini and Tomato Salad

Fresh Baked Bread

Nanaimo Bars

Sauvignon Blanc with Halibut or Pinot Noir with Salmon

I tried to include as many fresh ingredients as possible in the Days 1-4 menus.

Stuffed French Toast

Serves 5.

> 5 slices sourdough or other bread, 1-inch thick
> 3 bananas
> 3 eggs
> 1/2 cup milk
> 1 t vanilla (or 1/2 t Mexican, if possible)
> 1/4 cup oil
> 3/4 cup maple syrup

Insert small sharp knife in one side of each bread slice and form a pocket, leaving a 1-inch border. Halve bananas crosswise and then lengthwise. Stuff 2 pieces into each bread slice. Set aside. Whisk eggs, milk, and vanilla in shallow dish. Heat 1 tablespoon of oil in pan, more if needed. Dip bread slices in egg mixture and lift with spatula into hot oil and fry until brown on both sides, remove and serve with maple syrup.

Before Trip:

- Measure out 5 1-inch slices of bread and cut at the end of the 5 inches. Do not slice each piece individually yet. Put in a double bread wrapper and seal.
- Put milk in a plastic bottle and keep cold, or use powdered milk and put in ZLB with instructions.
- Take a small container of vanilla.
- Put maple syrup in plastic bottle and in a ZLB.
- Do the same for oil.

On Trip:

- Slice cantaloupe into 5 equal parts and put strawberries on top of each piece and let happy campers top it off with a few tablespoons of yogurt that you have set out.
- Prepare stuffed French toast recipe and begin cooking as people wander into the kitchen area.

Vegetable-Cheese Stuffed Pita

Serves 4-6.

1 large ripe avocado
1 T lemon juice
1/3 t garlic salt
1/4 t dried oregano
1/2 t Worcestershire Sauce
dash of red pepper sauce

1 tomato, diced
1 green onion, diced
1 small cucumber, diced
8 oz. French Cantal cheese (cut in small cubes)
¾ cup alfalfa sprouts or other greens
4-6 whole wheat pita bread (cut in half)

Cut avocado in half and remove the pit. Peel and chop the flesh coarsely. Combine with the lemon juice, garlic salt, oregano, Worcestershire, and red pepper sauce. Fill pita halves with avocado mixture. Combine tomato, green onion, cucumber, and cheese. Spoon over avocado filling and top with sprouts.

Before Trip:

- Put garlic salt, oregano, lemon juice, Worcestershire sauce, and red pepper sauce in a small container that does not leak.
- Wash and dry tomato, onion, and cucumber, put in ZLB.
- Put pita in ZLB.
- Put alfalfa sprouts in ZLB.
- If avocado is ripe, keep it in the cooler, if not, let it sit out a day or two.
- Put cheese in ZLB.
- Put pickles and peppers in separate ZLB.

On Trip:

- Before or after breakfast make filling for sandwiches and put in accessible cooler.
- Make sure your fruit, pickles, peppers, cookies, and pita are accessible for lunch.

Grilled Fish Steaks

Wrap 1/4 pound fish per person (I prefer 1-inch thick halibut or salmon steaks) in lightly buttered foil. If you have hearty eaters, you can go up to ½ pound per person. Place on grill over medium heat. Cook approximately 10 minutes per inch of thickness or until fish flakes. Open foil and spread with 1 to 2 tablespoons pesto butter per serving. Serve immediately.

Pesto Butter

Makes about 1 cup.

1 cup fresh basil leaves, firmly packed
1/2 T minced garlic (about 2 cloves)
1/4 cup pine nuts, toasted and cooled
1/8 cup olive oil
1/2 cup parsley

1/4 cup freshly grated Parmesan cheese
1/4 t salt
1/4 t pepper
1/2 cup unsalted sweet butter

Puree all ingredients in a blender or food processor. Put into a plastic container and freeze. Or roll into a log shape, wrap in plastic wrap, then in foil, label, date, and freeze. This butter will last 1 to 2 weeks in a cooler.

Parsleyed Rice

Makes 6 cups cooked rice, 6 to 8 portions.

4 cups water to which I add 4 chicken bouillon cubes
1 T salt if using just water without the cubes
2 cups uncooked long-grain rice (I use Jasmine or Thai rice)
8 T (1 stick) butter cut into 8 pieces (or squeeze margarine)
1 1/2 cups finely chopped Italian or other parsley, fresh is best

Bring the water or stock to a boil in a heavy pan. Stir in the rice and salt, return to a boil, reduce the heat to low, and cover tightly. Let the rice cook, undisturbed, for 25 minutes. Uncover the pan, add the butter and parsley (do not stir), and cover. Remove pan from heat and let stand for 5 minutes. Uncover pan, toss rice with a fork to mix in the butter and parsley, and serve.

Zucchini and Tomato Salad

Makes 6 servings.

2 small zucchini, about 3/4 lb
4 medium ripe tomatoes sliced 1/4 inch thick
1 small head lettuce (opt.)
salt and ground pepper to taste
1/4 cup finely chopped red onions (opt.)
1 T red wine vinegar
3 T olive oil
1/2 cup chopped basil or parsley (or 2 T dried)
4 oz. feta cheese

Trim the ends of the zucchini and cut them slightly on the diagonal into slices 1/4 inch thick. Drop the slices into boiling water, and let simmer for 1 minute. Drain immediately. The zucchini must retain a certain resilience and not be over-cooked. Let cool. Arrange the zucchini and tomato slices in an attractive pattern in a serving dish or on a bed of lettuce. Sprinkle with salt and pepper, onions, vinegar, oil, and basil or parsley on each layer, if there are multiple layers, and serve.

Fresh Baked Bread

This one is really easy. Buy a can of Pillsbury or Hungry Jack refrigerator whole wheat or French bread. Keep it in your cooler until you are ready to POP it and put in DO. Follow instructions on the can. Then voila! You have fresh baked bread.

Nanaimo Bars

Makes about 25 small squares.
These yummy goodies came from my husband's aunt, who lives in Nanaimo, Vancouver Island, B.C. Over the years, they have become known far and wide.

Bottom layer:
1/2 cup butter   1 egg
1/4 cup sugar   2 cups graham cracker crumbs
5 T cocoa   1 cup flaked coconut
1 t vanilla   1/2 cup chopped walnuts

Middle layer:
2 T butter   1 cup sifted confectioners sugar
1 1/2 T milk

Top layer:
4 sq. bittersweet chocolate   1 T butter

11

Place softened butter, sugar, cocoa, vanilla, and egg in a double boiler with water boiling. Stir well until butter is melted and mixture resembles custard. Combine crumbs, coconut, and nuts, blending well. Add to custard mixture. Pack evenly in 9-inch square pan (or 7x12). Cream 2 tablespoons butter. Add 1 1/2 T milk. Blend in 1 cup sifted confectioners sugar. Spread evenly over chocolate base. Put in freezer until slightly hardened, about 10 minutes. Then melt 4 squares bittersweet chocolate with 1 tablespoon butter and spread over white layer. When set, cut in small squares. Wrap in plastic and foil, label, and freeze.

Before Trip:

- Put nuts in ZLB.
- Double bag fresh fish in ZLB and put directly on ice in cooler or put in cooler with dry ice if this is to be a meal later on.
- Make pesto butter.
- Wash and dry zucchini and tomatoes, and put in ZLB.
- Combine vinegar, oil, chopped basil or parsley, salt and pepper in a small plastic bottle.
- Put rice and bouillon cubes with instructions in ZLB.
- Put 1 stick of butter in ZLB.
- Wrap fresh washed parsley for rice dish in paper towels and put in ZLB.
- Put bread in ZLB.
- Make Nanaimo bars.

On Trip:

- Set out nuts.
- Make sure your fish is thawed.
- Prepare zucchini and tomato salad, set aside.
- Make charcoal chimney fire.
- Make parsleyed rice.
- While rice is cooking, lightly oil the bottom and sides of a 12-inch DO.
- Pop open can of bread and put in DO on fire.
- If still frozen, set out Nanaimo bars. If not leave them in cooler and set out after dinner.
- When everything is 15 minutes from being done, grill the fish, and serve your meal with wine and pride.

Menu Two

Days 1 - 4

Breakfast

Apple or Cheese Blintzes

Rhubarb Strawberry Preserves and Sour Cream

Spicy Turkey Sausage

Lunch

Almond Chicken Salad Sandwiches

Dried Cranberries and Grapes

Pringles Potato Chips

Heath Bars

Dinner

Crackers and Cream Cheese with Peach Chutney or Pickapeppa Sauce

Honey Hoisin Chicken

Summer Squash with Lemon and Black Olives

Orange-Avocado Salad with Honey Dressing

Gingered Rhubarb-Apple Crisp

Pinot Gris (Pinot Grigio)

Apple or Cheese Blintzes

Makes about 18 blintzes.

For blintzes: 2 eggs   3/4 cup sifted flour
                     1 cup milk   2 T oil
                     1/2 t salt   2 T butter
                                           sour cream (opt.)

Beat eggs, milk, and salt together. Whisk in the flour, then oil until smooth. Chill 30 minutes. Heat a little butter in a 6-inch skillet. Pour about 2 tablespoons of the batter into it, tilting the pan to coat the bottom thinly. Brown on one side, then turn out onto a paper towel, browned side up. If you want to freeze these and assemble on your trip, cool the blintzes. Stack them with a piece of wax paper in between each one and wrap in plastic and then in foil and label. Do not freeze for more than 2 weeks.

For apple filling: 1 15-oz. can applesauce or,
                         1 1/2 cups chopped tart apple (1 large apple)
                         1/3 cup sugar
                         1/4 t nutmeg
                         2 T butter

Melt butter in pan, add apples, sugar, and nutmeg. Let simmer until slightly soft but still crunchy. Freeze in a ZLB.

For cheese filling: 1 lb ricotta cheese
                          1 egg
                          pinch of sugar
                          1/2 t vanilla
                          1/4 t cinnamon (opt.)

Mix all ingredients and beat until smooth. You can make this 1 or 2 days in advance but do not freeze by itself.

Final preparation: Place about 1 tablespoon of the filling, apple or cheese in the center of the blintz pancake. Roll over the base, flip over the sides and form the pancake into a "parcel" around the filling. Heat a little oil in a frying pan. Place the blintzes, seam side down, in the oil and fry for 4 or 5 minutes, turning them once. Or bake them in a DO. You can serve them with sour cream on the side. I prefer to assemble my blintzes ahead of time, freeze in a ZLB, and let them thaw on the trip. It saves time. Making some of each kind of blintz is easy, and your friends will be impressed with your efforts.

Rhubarb Strawberry Preserves

1/2 lb rhubarb, cut into 1-inch slices; or 1 1/2-lb package frozen sliced rhubarb
1 5-oz. jar red currant jelly
1/2 pint small strawberries, washed, hulled, and sliced

Put rhubarb and jelly in a large, heavy pot. Bring to a boil over high, stirring frequently. Reduce heat to moderately low, cover, and simmer 8 to 10 minutes, stirring occasionally until rhubarb is tender. Remove from heat. Mash rhubarb with a slotted spoon or potato masher. Add strawberries. Bring to a full, rolling boil over high heat; boil 1 minute. Remove from heat. Pour into glass jars. Cover and store in refrigerator until trip then put into plastic containers. Seal and label. This will keep 2-3 weeks in the refrigerator.

Spicy Turkey Sausage

I usually allow 1/4 pound sausage per person.
So easy. Buy your sausage, put in a ZLB, and freeze until trip.

Before Trip:

- Make apple and cheese blintzes and freeze.
- Make rhubarb strawberry preserves and keep in refrigerator in plastic container.

On Trip:

- Make sure your blintzes and sausages are thawed.
- Cook sausages in a skillet, or on a grill.
- Melt 1-2 tablespoons of butter in a skillet, add blintzes. Turn them only once until heated through, 10-20 minutes.
- Set out preserves and sour cream. Have yourself a cup of fresh brewed coffee until everything is ready to be served.

Almond Chicken Salad Sandwiches

Makes 6-8 sandwiches.

1 medium onion, peeled and quartered
1 large carrot, trimmed and cut into 2-inch pieces
1 med celery rib with leaves, cut into 2-inch pieces
1 bay leaf
1/4 t dried thyme
6 whole sprigs fresh parsley
1 t salt

10 whole black peppercorns
3 whole chicken breasts (about 3 lbs total)
2/3 cup loosely packed fresh parsley leaves
3/4 cup of sliced roasted almonds
2 medium shallots, peeled and halved
1 cup mayonnaise

Bring 4 quarts water to a boil in a large pot. Add the onion, carrot, celery, bay leaf, thyme, parsley, salt and peppercorns and simmer, uncovered for 15 minutes. Add chicken and simmer 20 minutes. Remove from heat and cool the chicken in broth to room temperature. Finely chop parsley leaves. Roast sliced almonds in the oven until lightly browned at 375° for about 5-10 minutes. Finely chop shallots. Remove chicken from broth and discard the skin and bones. Tear chicken into bite size pieces, and combine with mayonnaise, shallots and parsley. Add almonds just before serving. Taste for seasoning. Put in plastic container or ZLB and refrigerate. I use boneless chicken, which cuts down a few steps in preparation time.

Before Trip:

- Make almond chicken salad and store in refrigerator if you plan to eat it in 2-3 days.
- If not eating salad until later on trip (5-6 days), cook chicken, put in ZLB by itself and freeze; then right before trip chop parsley and put in ZLB. Put roasted almonds in ZLB.
- Wash and dry 1 piece lettuce per sandwich the day before you leave on your fabulous trip. Put lettuce in ZLB with a paper towel.
- Buy dried cranberries; these are wonderful if you can find them. If not use another dried fruit and put in ZLB. I usually buy 1 pound per 5-6 people. Be creative; buy a mixture of dried fruit.

On Trip:

- If chicken salad is not complete, finish making it before or after breakfast the day you want to eat it. Add roasted almonds and mix right before you serve.
- Set out chicken salad, bread, lettuce, dried cranberries, fresh grapes, and Pringles.
- After eating, pull candy bars from the cooler and yell "SURPRISE", and everyone will love you for the rest of the day, if not for the rest of the trip.

Crackers and Cream Cheese
with Peach Chutney or Pickapeppa Sauce

Serves 5.

> Crackers, your choice
> 8oz. package Cream Cheese
> Peach Chutney or Pickapeppa Sauce

Pour sauce over cream cheese on a plate. Put crackers in a nice dish and serve. This is easy and delicious.

Honey Hoisin Chicken

Serves 6.

4 1/2 t Hoisin or plum sauce   6 skinless chicken breast halves with or without bones
2 t honey   1/8 t salt
2 t rice vinegar   black pepper to taste
1/2 t cinnamon
generous 1/4 t crushed red pepper flakes
1/4 t vegetable oil, plus a little extra oil for the DO

Stir together the Hoisin sauce, honey, rice vinegar, cinnamon, crushed red pepper, and vegetable oil. Lightly oil a DO and put chicken in pan and brush with some of the Hoisin sauce mixture. Sprinkle with salt and pepper. Put on fire and bake, 350° if using an oven. After approximately 20 minutes brush on more sauce and continue to bake until the chicken starts to blister and brown. Do the same for grilling.

Summer Squash
with Lemon and Black Olives

Makes 6 servings.

10 brine-cured black olives (seedless if you can find them), rinsed and patted dry
3 small zucchini (about 1 lb), washed and ends trimmed
3 small yellow squashes (about 1 lb), washed and ends trimmed
2 T unsalted butter
salt and freshly ground black pepper
2 t grated lemon peel
1/2 cup grated Parmesan cheese (opt.)

Pit the olives and cut each one into 4 pieces. Set aside. Cut each squash lengthwise into quarters and remove seeds. Removal of seeds can be optional. Cut each strip on the diagonal into 1/4-inch pieces. Melt butter in a large skillet over medium-high heat. Add squash pieces, season with salt and pepper and cook, stirring often, until just tender, about 4 minutes. Stir in olives and heat through. Remove from heat, add lemon peel, Parmesan cheese, and toss well to mix. Taste for seasoning. Don't forget to let your friends know if you leave the seeds in the olives. No one wants a broken tooth.

Orange-Avocado Salad

Makes 6-8 servings.
This is a wonderful combination of fruit and vegetables. And the honey dressing gives it a delicious and unusual flavor.

> 1 lb spinach leaves or any type of lettuce
> 1 small red onion, peeled, thinly sliced
> 4 small seedless eating oranges
> 1 large avocado, firm but ripe, peeled, split vertically, pitted
> 2 t lemon juice

Wash spinach or lettuce and put in a bowl. Peel oranges and slice crosswise. Do the same with the avocado and sprinkle lemon juice on top. Arrange oranges overlapping slices in a circle on spinach or lettuce leaves, allowing 1-inch of green to show at edge of bowl. Arrange avocado slices in center of salad bowl. Tuck the onion slices into spaces between the oranges and avocados. I know, picky, picky, picky, but just think of the oohs and ahs when people see how creative you can be. Serve honey dressing separately.

Honey Dressing

Makes 3/4 cup dressing.

> 2 T fresh parsley leaves   3/4 t salt
> 1 T chopped onion   1/2 t Hungarian paprika
> 1 t Polish or other mustard   3 T honey
> 3 T cider vinegar   1 T lemon juice
> 1/3 cup oil

The easy way out. With metal blade in place, add parsley and onion to bowl of food processor. Process, turning machine on and off 6 times. Add remaining ingredients and process 10 seconds. Put in container and refrigerate. This will keep 1-2 weeks. The hard, grueling, old fashioned way. Do everything manually. This is also a great recipe for fruit salads.

Orange-Avocado Salad, Page 18

Summer Squash, Page 17

Gingered Rhubarb-Apple Crisp

Serves 6-8.

1/3 cup sugar
1/4 cup plus 1 T flour, divided
1 t peeled, grated fresh ginger
3 1/2 cups fresh or frozen rhubarb (about 14 oz.), sliced 1-inch thick
2 medium cooking apples (2 cups), peeled and cut into 1/2-inch cubes
1-2 T oil or vegetable cooking spray
1/3 cup firmly packed brown sugar
1/4 cup quick-cooking oatmeal, uncooked
2 T butter, melted

Combine sugar and 1 T flour in a medium bowl; cut in ginger with a fork until well-combined. Add rhubarb and apple; toss well. Spoon into a 10-inch DO coated with oil or cooking spray. Combine remaining 1/4 cup flour, brown sugar, and oatmeal in small bowl; add butter, tossing with a fork until well combined. Sprinkle over rhubarb. Put on fire for 20 to 30 minutes or until rhubarb is tender and you can not stand the aroma any longer. This also can be baked in a regular oven at 350° until brown and bubbly.

Before Trip:

- Put cream cheese in ZLB in refrigerator.
- Put crackers in ZLB.
- Put chutney in a plastic container and in a ZLB in refrigerator.
- Make honey Hoisin sauce and do the same as above.
- Buy, wash, and put chicken in ZLB and freeze.
- Make honey dressing and put in MSB. Keep refrigerated until trip. Lasts 1-2 weeks.
- Buy rhubarb day before trip. Wash, slice, and put in ZLB. Keep refrigerated. Use frozen rhubarb if you cannot find fresh. But...I have to warn you it is much better fresh.
- Mix dry ingredients for oatmeal topping and put in ZLB.
- Combine the 1/3 cup sugar and 1 T flour to go on rhubarb and apples. Put in ZLB.

On Trip: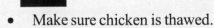

- Make sure chicken is thawed.
- Set out hors d'oeuvres.
- Make charcoal chimney fire for chicken and dessert.
- Prepare squash for cooking.
- Make orange-avocado salad, set aside.
- Baste chicken with honey Hoisin sauce and put on grill or in DO.
- While chicken is cooking, make rhubarb dessert.
- When chicken is done, remove, and put dessert in DO and start baking.
- Just before chicken is done, sauté squash. Serve everything at once. If you pull this meal off, I promise you will get rave reviews.

Menu Three
Days 1 - 4

Breakfast
Soft Tacos with Chorizo Mexican Sausage
Refried Black Beans
Homemade Chipotle Salsa

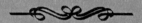

Lunch
Oriental Pasta Salad
Assortment of Gourmet Crackers/Bread
Crunch Bars

Dinner
Roasted Nut Mix
Beef and Zucchini Casserole
Carrot-Raisin Salad
Italian Bread with Herbs
Poppy Seed Cookies
Red Zinfandel

Soft Tacos

with Chorizo Mexican Sausage

Makes 5 tacos.

 6 oz. chorizo Mexican sausage, remove outside casing
 1 baked (slightly firm) potato, remove or leave skin on, diced into small pieces
 5 eggs
 5 (6-8 inch) flour tortillas
 1/4 cup grated cheese per taco
 1-2 T chipotle salsa per taco

In a skillet using medium heat, cook the sausage until it is done, drain off excess fat. Add potato and eggs and cook until eggs are firm. Wrap your tortillas in foil and heat 5 minutes on your grill in camp. Or in a skillet on a Coleman stove, or sometimes I wrap them in foil and steam them over my hot water for coffee. Put the above mixture in the tortillas, add cheese and roll up. I make my tacos at home, wrap in foil, put in a ZLB and freeze for 2-3 weeks before my trip. Do not add salsa at this time. Take on trip and let everyone add their own according to taste.

Refried Black Beans

Serves 4-6.

When I am running short on time I buy canned refried beans. All you have to do is heat them in a pan, serve with grated cheese and chopped onions on top, and add some salsa. Being from Texas we put salsa on just about everything. 1 16-oz. can refried black beans serves 3-4 people.

To make your own:

1 1/2 cups black beans or pinto beans	2 T chili powder
1 1/2 medium onions, chopped	1 T cumin
3 cloves garlic, minced salt to taste	12 cups water
3 jalapeno chile peppers, finely chopped (opt.)	1 bay leaf
2-3 T habanero pepper sauce, for those of you	

who really want a fiery taste. Keep the water handy.

Soak beans in water overnight first and drain. Put everything in a large pot. Bring to a boil. Reduce heat to maintain a gentle boil and cook for 2 to 3 hours uncovered or until beans are tender. Put 1/2 to 3/4 of the beans in a blender or food processor and blend until smooth. You can use a potato masher but it will take longer. Make sure your beans are not too watery when you add your blended beans to the large pot of remaining beans. Mix all beans together, put in MSB, and freeze. Lasts 4-6 months in freezer. When reheating you might want to add some water to thin the beans and make them more creamy. Adjust seasoning as needed.

Homemade Chipotle Salsa

Makes about 4 cups.

This recipe is to die for, really, it is so good. Chipotles are actually smoked, dried jalapeno chiles. They are hot with a wonderful smoky flavor. Chipotle chiles are usually canned in adobo sauce which I use in this recipe.

1 large can Italian plum tomatoes, drained
3 tomatoes, skinned and seeded
1/2 small onion, cut into pieces
3-4 pickled chipotle chiles
1 clove garlic
3 green onions, minced
1 T oregano
1 T rice vinegar

Open can of tomatoes and take out seeds with your fingers. Cut the fresh tomatoes into large pieces. Place all tomatoes, onion, chipotles, and garlic into a food processor fitted with the metal blade. Turn the machine on and off 3-4 times until you get a coarse puree. Put puree into a saucepan along with the rest of the ingredients and simmer for 15 minutes. Cool and refrigerate. Lasts 2 weeks in refrigerator.

Before Trip:

- Make soft tacos and freeze.
- Make black refried beans and freeze.
- Make chipotle salsa, put in plastic container and refrigerate.
- Buy Beano (opt.).

On Trip:

- Heat tacos on grill, baking sheet, or skillet on top of your camping stove over a low flame until hot inside. Or steam them over hot water.
- Heat refried beans in pan on stove.
- Set out chipotle salsa and Beano. Tell people to line up for a Tex-Mex experience.

Oriental Pasta Salad

Makes about 10 cups, 6-8 servings.

1 lb canned shrimp
5 dried black Chinese mushrooms (delete if you cannot find them)
8 oz. cooked udon noodles, in 3 1/2-inch lengths, or other Chinese noodles
8 oz. jicama, peeled, cut into match-like strips
4 oz. large fresh snow peas, cut into strips
1 large green pepper, cut into strips
8 oz. fresh mushrooms, stems trimmed, and sliced
3 large scallions, sliced
3 medium carrots, cut into match-like strips or grated
Oriental Vinaigrette (recipe follows)

Drain liquid off shrimp. Set aside. Soak the dried mushrooms in warm water to cover for 1/2 hour. Drain and squeeze out excess moisture. Cut off the stems and save for a soup or stock. Cut the caps into 1/8-inch strips with scissors; set aside. Prepare the Oriental Vinaigrette. Put the noodles in a 4-quart serving bowl, add the dressing and reserved mushroom strips and toss gently. Add the shrimp and vegetables to the noodles and toss gently. Can serve at room temperature. This can be made up 2 days in advance and kept refrigerated. You will really surprise your rafting buddies if you use fresh shrimp in this dish. If you dare to do this, buy fresh or frozen shrimp and sauté them in 2 T oil then follow recipe above. If using fresh or frozen shrimp it is best to serve it the day you make it or the day after.

Oriental Vinaigrette

Makes about 1 1/3 cups.

1/2 cup oil
1/2 cup white rice vinegar
1/4 cup water
2 T sugar
1 T five-spice powder, usually found in most grocery stores or a Chinese grocery. It consists of finely ground: 2 whole star anise, 1 t whole fennel seeds, 1 t whole cloves, a 2-inch stick cinnamon, and 1 T Szechuan peppercorns.
2 t soy sauce
1 1/2 t salt
1 1/2 t any hot mustard
1 t sesame oil
zest of one orange, grated
freshly ground black pepper

Put all ingredients into a blender or food processor and blend for 3 seconds. Put in plastic container until trip.

Crunch Bars

Makes 8-10 bars.
When I worked as waterfront director at a camp in Colorado, a colleague received a Care Package of these from her mother in Louisiana. I couldn't get enough of them.

1 1/2 cup graham cracker crumbs
1 can Eagle Brand milk
1 cup chocolate chips
1 cup butterscotch chips or other flavored chips
1 cup chopped English walnuts

Mix all ingredients and spread in well greased 9 inch square pan. Bake 30-35 minutes at 350°. Allow to cool 45 minutes. Cut, wrap in plastic, then foil, and freeze until trip. Can reheat or eat at air temperature. These bars are also good with a scoop of vanilla ice cream. And, yes I have had ice cream on a river trip.

Before Trip:

- Make oriental vinaigrette dressing and refrigerate. Can make ahead 1-2 weeks.
- Make oriental pasta 1 or 2 days before it is to be consumed. If making it on the trip, do it the day before, or before breakfast the morning of the day it is to be eaten.
- Buy crackers/bread.
- Make crunch bars.

On Trip:

- For this lunch remind everyone after breakfast that they will need a cup, spoon, or plate to eat their pasta salad.
- Set out salad, crackers/bread, and dig in.

Roasted Nut Mix

Makes 3 cups.
This is an exceptional nut mix because of the spices. It disappears very quickly.

1 cup each of pecans, almonds, walnuts
1 1/2 T minced herbs (such as rosemary, savory, thyme, and sage)
1/8 t chili pepper

1/8 cup maple syrup
1 T olive oil
salt and pepper to taste

Preheat oven to 350°. In a bowl, combine all ingredients except salt and pepper. Mix well. Spread nuts on a baking sheet and toast 15-20 minutes, or until browned, stirring occasionally. Season with salt and pepper and toss frequently until cooled. Store in an airtight container for up to 2 weeks.

Beef and Zucchini Casserole

Serves 5-6.

1 lb ground beef
5 1/2-oz. package Bisquick mix
1 cup small curd creamed cottage cheese
1/2 grated Parmesan cheese

3 or 4 small zucchini, cut into 1/4-inch slices
2 cups spaghetti sauce
1 egg

This is an easy one. Grease a 10 inch DO. Cook and stir ground beef in skillet until brown; drain. Place zucchini slices in single layer in DO; sprinkle with 1/4 cup Bisquick mix. Top with beef and spaghetti sauce. Mix remaining 1 cup Bisquick mix, cottage cheese and egg until soft dough forms; spread over sauce. Sprinkle with Parmesan cheese. Bake 375° for about 30 minutes on coals. Let stand 10 minutes before serving. If you prefer a meatless dish leave out the beef and add more vegetables. Also you can substitute the ground beef and spaghetti sauce by buying meat spaghetti sauce already in a jar, which will last longer.

Carrot-Raisin Salad

Serves 5-6.

4 cups grated carrots
1/2 cup raisins
1 1/2 t cinnamon
1/2 t vanilla

about 2 cups yogurt sweetened with 2 to 3 T honey
1/2 cup pineapple tidbits, drained
1/2 t nutmeg
chopped walnuts or pecans (opt.)

Combine all ingredients 2 to 3 hours before serving to allow flavors to blend. This can be made 1-3 days in advance and put in a plastic container or ZLB, and refrigerated until trip. To make this really fancy looking, set your salad on a bed of different kinds of lettuce or other greens, use your imagination.

Italian Bread with Herbs

Another one of those difficult time consuming recipes. Buy your bread and keep refrigerated. Cream 1/2 cup unsalted sweet cold butter and add 2-3 T of your favorite herb. I like to add fresh dill, parsley, chives, basil, cilantro, or tarragon, and sometimes I mash 1 or 2 cloves of garlic and add to butter. Experiment, it is fun. Roll your butter into a log, wrap in plastic, then in foil, and freeze until trip.

Poppy Seed Cookies

Makes 5 dozen.

1 cup sugar	1/2 t grated nutmeg
Peel of one orange	1 cup unbleached flour
1 egg yolk	1 cup cake flour
1 cup unsalted butter,	1/4 cup poppy seeds
softened and cut into 8 pieces	
1/2 t salt	

Combine sugar and orange peel in food processor and mince finely. Add yolk and process a few seconds. Add butter, salt, and nutmeg and mix until light and fluffy, about 1 minute. Add remaining ingredients and mix using 4-5 on/off turns. Be careful not to over process. Divide dough into 4 equal portions and set each portion on a sheet of plastic wrap. Shape dough into 2x4-inch cylinders. Wrap tightly in plastic wrap and chill until firm, about 1 hour. Dough can be frozen at this point. Cut each cylinder into 1/4-inch slices and set on baking sheets, 1 1/2 inches apart. Bake at 350°until edges are lightly browned, about 8 minutes. Transfer to wire rack and cool. These cookies can be made 1-2 months before a trip and frozen. Bake them 1-2 days before your trip to have wonderfully fresh cookies. This is one of my favorites and is always a crowd pleaser.

Before Trip:

- Make roasted nut mix.
- Brown ground beef and put in MSB in freezer with spaghetti sauce. You can also buy your spaghetti sauce in jars but make sure you transfer it to plastic containers or an MSB before the trip.
- Buy zucchini the day before your trip, wash, dry, and put in a ZLB.
- Put Bisquick in ZLB.
- Buy cottage cheese the day before your trip. Tape container shut with masking tape and put in ZLB. If you are short on room skip the container and dump the cottage cheese in a ZLB.
- The day before your trip crack the egg into a plastic container or MSB. Make sure they are tightly sealed, for if they leak...
- Put the Parmesan cheese in a ZLB.
- Make your carrot-raisin salad. Put the nuts in a ZLB and add right before you serve the salad.
- Buy bread and make butter log.
- Make cookies.

- Set out roasted nut mix.
- Start coals for DO.
- Make beef and zucchini casserole.
- Set out carrot-raisin salad.
- Slice Italian bread and spread each piece with the herb butter log and wrap in foil. You can put the bread on the grill and turn several times, or put it in a DO and bake. Do this about 10 to 15 minutes before your casserole is finished baking.
- It is nice to open red wine and let it breathe before dinner, but if your group of friends is anything like ours you had better hide it or you will not have any for your dinner.
- After dinner set out the cookies.

Menu Four

Days 1 - 4

Breakfast

Grapefruit

Eggs Benedict with Asparagus

Nutmeg Muffins with Honey Butter

Lunch

Eggplant Sandwiches with Tomato and Mozzarella Cheese

Pickled Cucumbers and Pickles

River Pound Cake

Dinner

Cream Cheese with Sun Dried Tomatoes and Balsamic Vinegar

Beef Stuffed Cabbage Rolls

Marinated Bean Salad

New Potatoes with Dill

Hot Rolls

Chocolate Crepes

Cabernet Sauvignon

Grapefruit

I feel a need to do some of that infamous Texas bragging. We do have the best Rio Star ruby red grapefruits you will ever sink your teeth into, I am serious. You have not lived a proper life until you have had a sweet Texas grapefruit. Of course you might have to come to Texas and go down to the Lower Rio Grande Valley, or The Valley, as we call it, but it is well worth the trip.

Eggs Benedict with Asparagus

Serves 3-4.

Want to impress your friends with ease? This is the breakfast for you. People like their eggs cooked a variety of ways; soft, hard, scrambled, etc. Take egg orders to please everyone. Put one slice of sourdough bread (warmed or toasted) on your plate. On top of this add a slice of ham which has been warmed in a skillet, fresh steamed asparagus (or canned asparagus heated), eggs, and top off with Hollandaise sauce. The sauce can be made with a packaged mix that is available in grocery stores. Just be sure you get the mix that says all you do is add water and cook. 1.6 ounces of mix makes 1 cup.

Nutmeg Muffins

Makes 12 regular muffins.

These muffins can be made in advance and frozen in a ZLB, reheated or eaten cold on a hot sunny morning. I prefer to make my muffins in a DO right before I serve them. There are few things better than having fresh baked goodies on any river trip.

2 cups white flour (or 1 cup white and 1 cup whole wheat)	1/4 t salt
2 T sugar or 2 T maple syrup	1 cup milk (or dry milk, 3 T per cup)
1 T baking powder	2 large eggs
1/2 t freshly grated, or 3/4 t ground nutmeg	3 T butter, melted

Thoroughly mix flour, sugar, baking powder, nutmeg, and salt in a large bowl. Whisk milk, eggs, and butter until well blended; pour over dry ingredients and fold in with a rubber spatula, just until dry ingredients are moistened. If making muffins at home, heat oven to 375°. Grease muffin cups, or use foil or paper baking cups. Bake 15 to 20 minutes, or until lightly browned and springy to the touch in the center. Turn out onto a rack. If making muffins in DO, grease 10-inch DO, pour in mixed ingredients and place over prepared coals. Bake 20-30 minutes.

Honey Butter

Makes about 1/3 cup, enough for 4-6 muffins.

Honey butter is delicious on just about any bread from toast to pancakes. This keeps indefinitely in the refrigerator.

> 4 T unsalted butter, at room temperature
> 1 T honey (try different honeys)

Beat butter and honey in a small bowl or mixer until fluffy and well mixed. Store tightly covered in plastic container until trip.

Before Trip:

- Buy ingredients for eggs benedict. Put each ingredient in a ZLB with the exception of the eggs (refer to eggs at the beginning of book).
- Make sure asparagus is washed and dried before putting in ZLB.
- Make muffins and freeze. Or measure dry ingredients, place in ZLB.
- Put butter in ZLB.
- Make honey butter and refrigerate.

On Trip:

- Cut each grapefruit in half. If you are really nice you will section each person's grapefruit.
- Make enough coals for toasting bread and baking muffins.
- Set out honey butter.
- Toast or warm sourdough bread on grill over coals, or wrap bread in foil and place over coals, or on camp stove over low heat.
- Mix and bake muffins in DO.
- Heat ham in skillet on low.
- Take egg orders.
- Steam asparagus.
- Make Hollandaise sauce.
- When muffins have finished baking, cut into pieces and serve with honey butter. While people are chowing down on muffins, assemble each person's eggs benedict.
- Afterward sit back and enjoy the rave reviews! You deserve it.

Eggplant Sandwiches
with Tomato and Mozzarella Cheese

Makes 4 large sandwiches.

1 eggplant (about l lb), skin peeled
salt for draining eggplant
1 1/2 cups fruity green olive oil, or just olive oil
2 small dried red chiles, I use chipotle peppers (smoked jalapenos)
2-3 whole garlic cloves, slightly crushed
3 T red wine vinegar
2 T dried oregano
1 T dried basil
1 T coarsely crushed black peppercorns
8 slices of sourdough or whole wheat bread or 4 large pita bread
1 large tomato
4 large slices of mozzarella cheese

Cut the peeled eggplant into 1/8-inch thick round slices. Arrange them in layers in a colander, salting heavily as you do so. Weight with a heavy plate or bowl and let stand for l hour. Whisk together remaining ingredients. Rinse eggplant slices well, pat them dry with paper towels, put in MSB and pour marinade over eggplant. Seal bag and let it marinate for 3 days, refrigerated, shaking it once a day to distribute marinade. Arrange eggplant, sliced tomato, a slice of mozzarella, and drizzle a little marinade on each sandwich. You can save the marinade for another use on your trip, e.g. meat, salads, vegetables.

Pickled Cucumbers and Pickles

This is another tough one. Go to your favorite grocery store and buy these items. Put them in plastic containers and label.

River Pound Cake

Serves 12.
This is a delicious moist pound cake that can be frozen.

1/2 lb (2 sticks) sweet butter	1 t vanilla
2 cups sugar	5 eggs
2 cups white flour	strawberries (opt.)
1 1/2 T fresh lemon juice	

Preheat oven to 350°. Grease and flour a 10-inch bundt or tube pan. Cream butter and sugar gradually; beat until fluffy. Sift flour and add to butter mixture. Stir just enough to blend. Add lemon juice and vanilla; stir well. Add eggs, one at a time, mixing well after each addition. Pour batter into the prepared bundt or tube pan. Bake for 1 hour and 15 minutes, or until a cake tester inserted into the center of the cake comes out clean. (After 30 minutes, cover cake closely with aluminum foil.) When cake is done, cool in its pan on a cake rack for 10 minutes. Remove from pan and cool completely. Cut cake into slices, wrap in plastic wrap then foil. Put in ZLB, label, and freeze until trip. You can serve this cake with fresh strawberries or any good canned berries.

Before Trip:

- Make marinated eggplant.
- Buy tomato, wash, and put in ZLB the day before your trip. Do the same for mozzarella cheese.
- Buy bread and put in ZLB in refrigerator.
- Buy pickled items and put in plastic containers.
- Make pound cake and freeze. If you run out of time
  you can always buy a Sara Lee pound cake. They are very good. Be sure you put it in a ZLB.

On Trip:

- Drain liquid off eggplant after breakfast.
- For lunch set out eggplant, sliced tomato, sliced mozzarella cheese, pickled items, and sliced bread.
- Let everyone make their own sandwich.
- Set out pound cake and fresh strawberries if you have them.

Cream Cheese

with Sun Dried Tomatoes and Balsamic Vinegar

Serves 4-6.

8-oz. cream cheese
8-oz. sun dried tomatoes in olive oil and herbs
¼ cup capers
1/4 cup thick semi-sweet Balsamic vinegar, you will need to ask your grocer since there are many Balsamic vinegars
crackers

Set out your block of cream cheese and pour the rest of the ingredients over the cheese. It really makes a difference if you can find a semi-sweet Balsamic vinegar.

Beef Stuffed Cabbage Rolls

Serves 8 (2 rolls per person).

1 large head cabbage, cored
3 T butter
2 medium onions, chopped
1 lb lean ground beef, veal, or other meat
1 cup cooked white or brown rice, I like Basmati rice
1/2 cup seedless dark raisins
1 1/2 t allspice

1 28-oz. can tomatoes
1 8-oz. can tomato sauce
1 6-oz. can tomato paste
1 t salt
1/2 t garlic salt
1 t thyme
1 cup sour cream or plain yogurt

In a large pot, steam the cabbage for 10 minutes or until the leaves are softened enough to peel away. Cool, separate leaves, gently shake off moisture, and set aside. Melt butter in a skillet and sauté onions until they are golden. Brown the beef and put into a bowl. Remove half the onions to the bowl containing the ground beef. Mix in the rice, raisins, and allspice gently with your hands. To the remaining onions in the skillet, add the tomatoes and juice, tomato sauce, tomato paste, salt, and seasonings. Simmer for 15 minutes. Place a small amount of meat mixture on each cabbage leaf. Fold leaf over to enclose meat and, starting at the stem end, roll up. Cool cabbage rolls and gently put into a ZLB. Put tomato mixture into an MSB, seal and label. Put both items in freezer until trip. On your trip, thaw and place rolls, seam side down, in a greased DO. Cover with tomato mixture and bake, for 50-60 minutes at 350°. Serve with sour cream/yogurt.

Wine Anyone? (James Machin)

Hot Rolls, Page 35

Marinated Bean Salad

Serves 10-12.

> 1 can (about 1 lb) each of white kidney beans, garbanzo beans, red kidney beans, baby lima beans, and black-eyed peas
> 1/2 lb fresh green beans, or half green and half yellow wax beans, steamed, cooled, and cut into 2-inch lengths
> 1 small red onion, chopped
> 2/3 cup olive oil
> 2/3 cup sharp wine or cider vinegar
> salt to taste and lots of fresh ground pepper
> 2 T sugar
> chopped fresh herbs, basil or mint (opt.)

Drain canned beans, rinse thoroughly with water, and drain again. Toss in a bowl with fresh beans and chopped onion. Mix the rest of the ingredients to make the dressing, and pour it over the beans. Toss until everything is thoroughly combined and then refrigerate. You can make this up 2-3 days before your trip. Drain off most of the liquid the day before your trip and put in a ZLB and put back in refrigerator.

New Potatoes with Dill

Serves 8.

> 2 lbs small new (red) potatoes   salt (opt.)
> 5 T butter   pepper to taste, fresh ground
> 3 T fresh or dry dill, fresh for best results

Boil potatoes in camp until fully cooked but not falling apart. Drain water, add butter, dill, and spices. Eat! Make sure your potatoes are washed and kept dry before your trip.

Hot Rolls

Allow 2 rolls per person.

Easy times are here again. Buy the Pillsbury (or your favorite) refrigerator rolls. Put the cans in a ZLB and keep in your cooler until you are ready to POP rolls. Put in a lightly greased DO One stick of butter is plenty for 12 people. These bake in 5-10 minutes so keep a sharp eye on them. Put 8-10 rolls in a 10-inch DO, and 12-16 rolls in a 12-inch DO.

Chocolate Crepes

Makes 12 crepes.
One crepe per person is plenty since they are so intense. Besides, it is better leaving them begging for more.

2 eggs
1/2 cup flour
1/4 cup sugar
2 T unsweetened cocoa
1 cup milk

1 T butter, melted
1 t vanilla
butter for frying
Quick-and-Easy Chocolate Mousse

Crème Anglaise, Raspberry Sauce, or Hot Fudge Sauce (pick and make your favorite topping, but I must warn you that if you try all three the choice will be difficult, as they are all delicious).

With blender (do not use food processor, because the batter is so thin it will create a mess): combine first 7 ingredients and mix on low speed about 30 seconds just until combined; do not over blend. Or with electric mixer: Combine eggs and flour. Add sugar and cocoa. Pour in milk gradually, beating continuously and scraping sides of bowl to blend. Add butter and vanilla and beat until well mixed, no lumps in batter. Allow batter to stand covered 1 hr. before making crepes. Place 8-inch crepe pan or skillet over high heat and brush lightly with butter. When butter is sizzling but not brown, pour about 1/8-1/4 cup batter into pan. Quickly lift pan off heat and swirl to coat bottom of pan. Return to heat and cook about 1 minute, or until bottom darkens slightly and looks dry. Watch carefully, since both cocoa and sugar can cause crepes to burn easily. Turn crepe onto paper towel. Continue until all batter is used, brushing pan with butter as needed. When crepes are cooled, place about 1 heaping tablespoon of mousse on each and roll cigar-fashion. Place seam side down on baking sheet and freeze. When firm, wrap carefully in plastic. Put in ZLB and return to freezer until trip. These will keep up to 3-4 days in your cooler. Just be sure you put them in a place where they will not get squashed or you will be faced with a gooey mess.

Quick and Easy Chocolate Mousse

When filling the crepes with this yummy stuff, be generous.

2 cups semisweet chocolate (chips or chopped bars)
1 1/2 t vanilla
pinch salt

1 1/2 cups whipping cream, heated to
boiling point
6 egg yolks

Combine chocolate, vanilla, and salt in blender or food processor, fitted with steel blade, and mix 30 seconds. Add boiling cream and continue mixing 30 seconds more or until chocolate is completely melted. Add yolks and mix about five seconds. Transfer to bowl and allow to cool.

People will not believe that you are actually serving chocolate crepes for dessert on a raft trip. Watch their eyes bulge!

Crème Anglaise

This is wonderful stuff! One of my all time favorites.

4 egg yolks	1 t vanilla
1/2 cup sugar	1 1/2 cups half-and-half

Combine yolks and sugar in small bowl. Add vanilla and beat until light and fluffy. Place half-and-half into a 2-quart saucepan. Bring to a boil over high heat. Beating constantly, very slowly pour hot half-and-half into egg mixture. Transfer to saucepan and stir constantly over low heat about 20 minutes, or until custard coats back of metal spoon. This can be made 2-3 days before trip and sealed in an MSB. Keep refrigerated until you are ready to use. This can be served warm or cold over crepes. Crème Anglaise may be reheated in a pan placed over hot water. Beat constantly until heated, do not let boil.

Raspberry Sauce

Makes 1 cup.

10 oz. frozen raspberries	1 T lemon juice
1/3 cup seedless raspberry jam	1/4 cup Framboise (raspberry liqueur)

Place ingredients in bowl of a food processor or blender and process smooth. This can be made up 1 or 2 weeks in advance. Put in a MSB, label, and refrigerate. When serving cut a very small corner off the bag and drizzle on crepe.

Old Fashioned Hot Fudge Sauce

Makes 2/3 cup.
This is enough to drizzle over 12 crepes.

2 1-oz. squares unsweetened chocolate	1/2 t vanilla, or 1 T rum
4 T maple syrup (the best), or 1/2 cup corn syrup	1 t butter
salt to taste	

Melt chocolate in top of double boiler or pan over hot, but not boiling, water. Stir in maple or corn syrup. Remove from heat. Add salt, butter, vanilla or rum. Put in a plastic container or MSB, label, and refrigerate. This can be made 3 weeks in advance. Keep in cooler on trip. When ready to serve put bag in pan of water over low heat until warm. When serving cut a small corner off the bag and drizzle on crepe. This is my favorite hot fudge sauce. Try it you will love it.

Before Trip: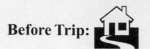

- Buy cream cheese, sun dried tomatoes, Balsamic vinegar, and crackers.
- Make beef stuffed cabbage rolls.
- Make marinated bean salad.
- Buy Pillsbury rolls.
- Make chocolate crepes and sauce.
- Buy dry ice for cooler, if needed.

On Trip:

- Make sure everything is thawed out, with the exception of crepes, the night before you prepare the meal.
- Make enough coals for 1 12-inch DO (for cabbage rolls) and 1 other DO for Pillsbury rolls (size of DO depends on number of rolls, refer to recipe).
- Make cream cheese appetizer.
- When coals are ready put cabbage rolls and their tomato sauce in DO and bake until hot, approximately 35 to 45 minutes.
- Pop open rolls and put in other DO and bake 20-30 minutes, or until you smell the wonderful aroma.
- Make new potatoes.
- Put marinated bean salad in a serving dish.
- Open wine to breathe.
- When everything is ready, set out buffet style and enjoy the fruits of your labor.
- After dinner when everyone is taking it easy, serve your luscious dessert.

Menu Five

Days 1 - 4

Breakfast

Homemade Crunchy Granola

Lemon Nut Bread

Cottage Cheese with Fresh Fruit

Lunch

Broccoli Fettuccine Salad

Assortment of Crackers and Cheese

Chocolate Chunk Oatmeal Cookies

Dinner

New Wave Guacamole and Tortilla Chips

Chicken Enchiladas with Green Sauce

Refried Two Tone Beans

Mexican Rice

Pralines

Gars, short for Margaritas

Homemade Crunchy Granola

Serves 10.
This is the best granola recipe I've ever made out of over 10 recipes.

Heat 6 cups of old fashioned cooking oats in an ungreased 13x9 inch pan in preheated 350° oven for 20 minutes, at least once.

Add: 3/4 cup wheat germ
1/2 cup coconut (opt.)
1/3 cup sesame seeds
1 1/2 cup chopped pecans

Slowly stir in: 1/2 cup vegetable oil
1/3 cup maple syrup or honey (or 1/2 cup brown sugar)
2 T molasses
1 1/2 t vanilla

Stir until all ingredients are well moistened. Bake in 350° oven until slightly brown, about 20-30 minutes. Stir often to insure even browning. Cool. Add 1 cup raisins, or dried cranberries, cherries, or blueberries. Store in a ZLB in refrigerator up to 1 month. This does not require refrigeration on your raft trip. I have tried plenty of granola recipes and this is by far the best and easiest to prepare.

Lemon Nut Bread

Makes 2 loaves.

2 cups sugar	2 t baking powder
1 cup butter	1 1/4 cups milk
4 egg yolks	grated peel of 2 lemons
3 1/4 cups flour	1 cup finely chopped nuts, any type of roasted nut
1 t salt	4 egg whites

Cream sugar and butter together well. Beat in egg yolks. Sift dry ingredients together and add alternately with milk. Mix well. Add lemon peel and nuts. Beat egg whites until stiff and fold into batter. Grease and flour 2 9x5x3-inch loaf pans and divide batter between them. Bake at 350° for 55-60 minutes.

Topping: juice of 2 lemons
1/4-1/2 cup sugar, or 1/4 cup maple syrup

Mix topping ingredients and spoon over bread. Leave bread in pans for 1 hour. Turn out of pans and cool completely on racks. Wrap in plastic, put in ZLB, label and freeze until trip.

Cottage Cheese with Fresh Fruit

Serves 6-8.
This is great to serve on a hot sunny morning such as on the Grand Canyon in the summertime.

1 24-oz. large curd cottage cheese
1 lb fresh strawberries or other berries, or a mixture of your favorite fruits

Put your cottage cheese container in a ZLB before trip and keep refrigerated. Wash, dry well, and hull strawberries the day before your trip. Put in a ZLB and refrigerate. On your river trip, put cottage cheese in a serving dish and decorate with your fruit. Be creative, make a face, randomly toss the fruit in, write a mysterious message, pile the fruit in the center, or put it on the side and let everyone else be creative.

Before Trip:

- Make granola.
- Make lemon bread.

On Trip:

- Set out granola with milk.
- Set out lemon bread, slice it and arrange on a serving dish.
- Set out cottage cheese and fruit.

Broccoli Fettuccine Salad

Serves 10.
This is another good dish on a blistering hot day.

> l bottle Italian Season dressing
> 2 large bunches of broccoli (flowerettes only), blanched
> 1 1/2 cup roasted sunflower seeds
> 1 pint cherry tomatoes, halved
> 3/4 cup raisins
> 1 3/4 lbs cooked fettuccine

Mix all ingredients. Pour as much dressing as you like on your salad. The flavor is enhanced if you let the salad sit overnight in the cooler or refrigerator.

Chocolate Chunk Oatmeal Cookies

Makes 16 cookies.
These are simply scrumptious.

1 1/4 cups unbleached flour
3/4 t baking powder
1/2 t baking soda
1/2 t salt
1 1/2 cups rolled oats or quick oats
1 cup pecans, toasted and chopped

1 cup dried cherries, chopped coarse
4 oz. bittersweet chocolate, chopped into chunks
12 T unsalted butter, softened
1 1/2 cups packed brown sugar, preferably dark
1 large egg
1 t Mexican vanilla

Heat oven to 350°. Mix first 4 ingredients in a bowl. Stir oats, pecans, cherries, and chocolate in second bowl. In a mixer, beat butter and sugar about 1 minute, until there are no more lumps. Add egg and vanilla and beat until fully incorporated. Add flour mixture and blend just until combined. Add oat mixture until just incorporated. Make sure all dough is mixed with no flour pockets. Roll dough in palm of hands and form 16 balls. Stagger 8 balls on each baking sheet, spacing about 2 1/2 inches apart. Gently press each dough ball to 1 inch thickness. Bake 20-22 minutes. You might want to rotate the cookie sheet, check after 12 minutes. The cookies are done when they are medium brown and edges have begun to set but centers are still soft. Do not overbake. Cool cookies on baking sheets on wire rack 5 minutes. Transfer to wire rack to finish cooling. Sometimes I make smaller cookies and cut the baking time in half. These cookies keep for 4 to 5 days stored in an airtight container or ZLB. They become chewy after a day or so but are still really tasty.

Before Trip:

- Buy Italian dressing and put in plastic container.
- Buy broccoli 2 days before trip, blanch, and put in ZLB.
- Buy cherry tomatoes 2 days before trip if they are already ripe. If not, you can buy them earlier and let them ripen on the trip. Wash, dry, put in ZLB.
- Buy raisins and put in ZLB.
- Buy fettuccine. Put in ZLB.
- Buy crackers (5-6 crackers per person). Put in ZLB.
- Buy cheese (1 lb for 10 people). Put in ZLB.

On Trip:

- Make sure everyone keeps out a fork and plate for lunch.
- Mix salad the night before so that the flavors have a chance to blend. Put in ZLB in an accessible lunch cooler.
- At lunch set out pasta salad, crackers, cheese, and cookies.

New Wave Guacamole

and Tortilla Chips

Serves 8.

4 large avocados, sliced into chunks (bite size)
1 large lime, or 1/4 cup lime juice
salt (opt.)
2 cups sour cream
1 8-oz. jar salsa
1 cup sharp cheddar cheese, grated
1 large bag tortilla chips

Let chunks of avocado sit in lime juice and a pinch of salt for 5-10 minutes, drain. Arrange all ingredients, with spoons, individually on a serving platter and let everyone choose how they want to load up their tortilla chips.

Gars (Short For Margaritas)

Makes 2 drinks apiece for 8 people.

Gars is how we refer to these Mexican cocktails. You can buy this as a mix. Or you can use my husband's authentic recipe, which is not for he/she who has a weak spirit or stomach He uses the 1,2,3 system.

1 cup plus 3 T Triple Sec. Do not use Cointreau or Grand Marnier; they are not sweet enough.
2 cups fresh squeezed lime juice or Real Lime juice, do not use Rose's lime juice or limeade (too sweet)
3 cups Tequila
salt for rim (opt.)

Chicken Enchiladas

with Green Sauce

Serves 8,
This recipe is well worth the effort if you enjoy good sauces on your enchiladas.

2 lbs skinless, boneless chicken breasts
2 to 3 celery stalks, cut into 1-inch chunks

1 onion, cut into large chunks
salt and pepper

Sauce:
1 quart chicken stock
2 lbs tomatillos, peeled
5 fresh serrano or jalapeno chiles,
seeds and pith removed, minced
2 garlic cloves, minced
1 onion, diced
1/2 bunch cilantro, minced (opt.)

1/4 t oregano
1/4 t freshly ground black pepper
pinch of sugar
pinch of salt
1 T butter
1 T flour

Filling:
2 green bell peppers, diced
2 onions, diced
2 large tomatoes, peeled and diced

3 canned large whole green peeled chiles,
seeded and diced (Hatch chiles are good)
chicken stock (opt.)
salt and pepper

16 corn or flour tortillas
16 thin slices Monterey Jack cheese
sour cream, yogurt, and black olives for garnish (opt.)

Place chicken in large pot and cover with water. Add celery, onion, salt and pepper and cook until chicken is tender, about 30 minutes. Remove chicken from broth and set aside to cool. Strain broth and reserve for sauce.

For sauce: Combine all ingredients except butter and flour in large saucepan. Bring to boil over medium heat, stirring occasionally and skimming off foam as it rises to surface. Reduce heat and simmer, stirring occasionally, until sauce is consistency of puree (about 1 hour), gently piercing tomatillos with a fork as they become soft. Strain sauce and return to pan. Combine butter and flour to form a paste. Add to sauce and cook over medium heat until sauce returns to boil and thickens slightly. Set aside and keep hot.

For filling: Combine peppers, onion, tomatoes and chiles in large skillet. Place over medium heat and cook until soft, stirring constantly and moistening with chicken stock if necessary. Shred cooled chicken. Add to filling and cook a few minutes more. Season with salt and pepper to taste.

To assemble: Dip each tortilla into green sauce. Place 1/4 cup filling in each tortilla, roll up and place seam side down on a cookie sheet. When you have rolled all enchiladas, put cookie sheet in the freezer for 30-40 minutes, until hard. Remove cookie sheet and gently put enchiladas in ZLB. After green sauce has cooled put in MSB and label.

Refried Two Tone Beans

1 16-oz. can serves 3-4 people.

The easy way out is to buy spicy refried pinto and black beans in a can. Just heat them up when you are ready to eat them. Or refer to Menu 3, Days 1-4 for refried beans.

Mexican Rice

Serves 4-6.

1 cup Basmati or long grain rice	2 tomatoes, peeled and chopped
1 garlic clove	1 cup water
1/2 salt	1 cup chicken broth
2 T oil	1/3 cup frozen peas
1 small onion, chopped	1 carrot, peeled, diced

Rinse rice in hot water, then cold water. Drain. Set aside. Mash garlic with salt to make a paste. Set aside. Heat oil in large, heavy saucepan. Add rice. Cook and stir over medium heat until lightly browned. Add onion and garlic paste. Cook and stir until onion is soft. Add tomatoes. Cook and stir until tomatoes are softened and blended into rice mixture. Add water. Cover and simmer until water is absorbed, about 10-20 minutes. Stir in broth and 1/2 t salt. Cover and simmer again until most of the liquid is absorbed, about 3-5 minutes. Reduce heat to low and steam until rice is tender, about 30-40 minutes. After rice has completely cooled add the peas and carrots. Put in a ZLB, label and freeze until trip.

Pralines

Various pralines are available on the market, but a unique and excellent one is the "Texas Chewie" Pecan Praline from Lammes Candies, in my home town of Austin, Texas. These last a long time. You won't be disappointed. We took boxes of these on treks to Mt. Everest and the Swiss Alps. They lasted four weeks and were a huge hit as part of our Thanksgiving feast at Mt. Everest base camp. Order at http://www.lammes.com/.

Before Trip:

- Make enchiladas and green sauce.
- Make Mexican rice.
- Make Mexican cookies or buy pralines.

On Trip:

- Make sure everything is thawed out the day before you prepare your dinner.
- Prepare coals for baking enchiladas.
- Have your designated bartender begin making margaritas while you make the guacamole.
- Serve drinks and set out guacamole and chips.
- Put enchiladas in DO and start baking.
- Heat rice and beans in pans on stove.
- Arrange cookies or pralines on serving dish.
- You will find that after a few stiff margaritas that everyone will no doubt think you are the best Mexican chef that ever walked the earth. So have fun with your happy friends.

Menu Six

Days 1 - 4

Breakfast

Hot Bagels with Honey Cream Cheese and Preserves

Prosciutto with Melon

Yogurt

Lunch

Curried Lentils in Pineapple with Chutney

Carrot Sticks and Pickles

Assorted Nuts

Ginger Cookies

Dinner

Vermont Cheddar on Crackers with Cranberry Sauce or Chutney

Maple Syrup-Mustard Glazed Chicken

Beet and Roquefort Salad with Walnuts

Lipton Noodles and Sauce

Chomeur

Zinfandel or Grenache

Hot Bagels

I usually allow 2 bagels for men and 1 for women. Sorry girls, I do not want to sound sexist, but according to my experience men generally eat more than women. You can prepare hot bagels three ways. Make hot coals and put split bagels on the grill until toasted. Or wrap them in foil and put them over steaming water on your stove. You can toast on a griddle or use a camp toaster.

Honey Cream Cheese

Serves 8.

You can serve your honey and cream cheese separately. Or you can mix (before trip) 6 T honey with two 8-ounce packages of cream cheese.

Prosciutto with Melon

Serves 8.

> 3/4-1 lb prosciutto, sliced
> 2 cantaloupe or honeydew melons

Set out prosciutto and melon cut in chunks. People can wrap their chunks of melon in the prosciutto and eat. If you have never tried this, you should, it is tasty and easy. This is one of the items that Swiss people have for breakfast along with tasty homemade preserves and crusty bread.

Before Trip:

- Day before trip buy fresh bagels if possible and put in a ZLB and refrigerate.
- Mix up honey and cream cheese 4 days before trip. Put in plastic container, refrigerate.
- Buy preserves and put in plastic container.
- Day before trip buy prosciutto and melon. Put prosciutto in ZLB, refrigerate. Melon can go in cooler as is.

On Trip:

- Prepare hot bagels.
- Set out honey cream cheese and preserves.
- Cut up melon and set out with prosciutto.
- Set out yogurt.

Curried Lentils in Pineapple with Chutney

Serves 5.

1 pineapple, or two 16-oz. cans pineapple
1 1/2 T butter
2 1/2 cups cooked lentils (about 1 cup dried)
1/2 t salt
3/4 t cumin seeds or 1 t cumin spice
1/2 t mustard seed or 3/4 t dry mustard
1/2 t turmeric
1/2 t ground coriander
pinch of cayenne
2 tomatoes, firm and large (opt.)
1 6-8 oz. jar of chutney

Vinaigrette Sauce:

2 T white wine vinegar
6 T olive oil
1 t Worcestershire sauce
1 t Dijon mustard (or other)
1 clove garlic
1/4 cup dry white wine
salt and fresh ground pepper

I use canned pineapple because it takes up less room and is easier to store. If using fresh pineapple do the following. Cut the top off, cut off the outside, slice down the middle, and core. If using cumin and mustard seeds, heat the butter in a skillet and add the spices to it. After a few minutes, add the cooked, drained lentils and mix them well with the heated spices. If not using cumin and mustard seeds, add all spices to drained lentils and simmer for 1-2 minutes. Cool. Prepare the vinaigrette sauce by putting all ingredients in a blender and mixing. Pour sauce over lentils and toss. Put in MSB and freeze until trip. Right before I serve this lentil dish I drain or let someone drink the canned pineapple juice, in our group there is always a taker. Then I cut up the already washed fresh tomatoes and add the lentils and pineapple. Serve with your favorite chutney.

Carrot Sticks and Pickles

Pickles can be bought at the store and put in a plastic container or MSB with its juice. One 16 ounce jar is enough for 10 people.

On short trips I wash, peel, and quarter my carrots the day before my trip. I seal them in an MSB half full of water and keep them refrigerated for freshness. You will be amazed at how many people who normally do not eat carrot sticks will hunker down on these crisp little sticks. These also make great snacks, and you can use the leftover water to drink or cook with, or for soups. I usually use 6 medium sized carrots for 10 people.

Assorted Nuts

One can of 12-16 ounces of nuts is plenty for 10 people.

Ginger Cookies

Makes 4 dozen.

> 2 1/4 cups white flour
> 1 1/2 t baking soda
> 1/2 t salt
> 1 piece peeled fresh ginger, about l x l x 1/2 inch
> 3/4 cup (1 1/2 sticks) unsalted butter, at room temperature, cut into 6 pieces
> 1 cup firmly packed dark brown sugar
> 1/4 cup molasses
> 1 large egg
> 1/2 cup blanched whole almonds

You can mix this recipe by hand, food processor, or mixer. If using a food processor, use the metal blade to mix the flour, baking soda and salt, turning the machine on and off 2 or 3 times. Set aside. With the machine running, drop the ginger through the feed tube and process until minced. Add the butter and turn the machine on and off 6 to 8 times to blend. Add the sugar, molasses and egg and process until smooth, about 15 to 20 seconds, stopping twice to scrape down the bowl. Add the flour mixture and turn the machine on and off 3 or 4 times, until the flour just disappears. Carefully remove the dough, wrap it in plastic wrap and refrigerate at least 2 hours or overnight. Preheat the oven to 350°. Form the dough into walnut-sized balls and place 2 inches apart on a lightly greased baking sheet. Press a blanched almond in the center of each. Bake l0 to l2 minutes in the lower third of the preheated oven, until firm to the touch. The cookies may be frozen for up to 2 months.

Before Trip: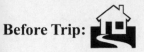

- Make curried lentils.
- Buy tomatoes the day before your trip. Wash and put in a ZLB.
- Buy chutney and put in an MSB or plastic container.
- Do carrot sticks and pickles.
- Make and freeze ginger cookies.

On Trip:

- Keep out a bowl or a few ZLBs for mixing the lentils.
- Add chunks of drained pineapple and fresh quartered tomatoes to the curried lentils.
- Set out chutney.
- Set out carrot sticks and pickles. I like to arrange these on some sort of serving dish.
- Set out nuts.
- Set out ginger cookies.
- Everyone dig in.

Vermont Cheddar on Crackers
with Cranberry Sauce or Chutney

I think the white Vermont sharp cheddar is the best, with New York a close second. You can always buy cranberry sauce or cranberry chutney already made, but I prefer to buy the fresh cranberries in the bag, follow the instructions on the package for cooking, oh so easy and more delicious. It will last in an MSB up to one month when refrigerated. The above combination provides a nice sharp but sweet flavor. Simple but tasty.

Maple Syrup-Mustard Glazed Chicken

Serves 4.

4 skinless chicken breast halves on the bone
2 T Dijon mustard
2 T maple syrup or dark brown sugar
2 t cider vinegar
1 t vegetable oil

Stir together the mustard, maple syrup, vinegar, and oil. Line your DO with aluminum foil and place the chicken in the pan. Brush with some of the glaze. Bake 40-50 minutes, brushing occasionally with some of the glaze. The last 2 minutes of baking load all the coals that were underneath the DO on top of the DO to brown chicken as much as possible. Sometimes it takes more than 2 minutes. Be patient, for it is good.

Beet and Roquefort Salad with Walnuts

Serves 6-8.
I know this salad sounds a little unusual but it really is good because of the different flavors and textures. It also keeps well. So if you do not mind having red hands for a day cutting up beets, I think you will enjoy this salad, especially you red hot beet lovers.

8-10 medium-sized beets
3 T red wine vinegar
3 T walnut oil, it is slightly on the expensive side but the flavor is superb.
1/2 cup shelled walnut halves, toasted
1/8-1/4 lb of Roquefort cheese
fresh ground black pepper

Wash beets well, and trim stems and roots without piercing the skin. Drop the beets into a large kettle of boiling salted water and cook until tender, 20 to 40 minutes, depending on beet size. Drain, cool, and peel beets, and cut into julienne strips. In a mixing bowl, toss the beets gently with the vinegar and walnut oil. Taste and add more of either if you like; there should be just enough to coat the beets. Put the beet mixture in a ZLB or MSB. Put Roquefort in ZLB. Put walnuts in ZLB. Keep beets and Roquefort in refrigerator. I would recommend making this 1-2 days before a trip. When ready to serve, toss the walnuts with the chilled beets and arrange in a serving dish. Sprinkle with the Roquefort and black pepper.

Lipton Noodles and Sauce

Serves 4.

This is exactly what it says it is, a Lipton Noodle sauce dish. Pick one up at your local grocery store and follow the instructions on the package. You will need milk and butter for this recipe. I usually buy the Alfredo package. Very easy and tasty on a raft trip.

Chomeur

Serves 8.
Chomeur is a type of pudding-cake, baked in a rich caramel sauce. People can't believe eating this on a raft trip because it is absolutely delicious and easy to make. You feel as though you are dining at a fancy restaurant.

1 1/2 cups light brown sugar, firmly packed	1/2 cup milk
1 cup milk	1 cup flour
3 T butter, chilled, cut into bits	1 t baking powder
1 egg, lightly beaten	1 t vanilla
3 T sugar	whipped cream (opt.)
2 T melted butter	

In a 12-inch DO combine brown sugar, 1 cup milk, and 3 T butter. In a mixing bowl, combine egg, sugar, and melted butter. This is the sauce. Add ½ cup milk and stir well. Sift together flour and baking powder into into egg-milk mixture and mix. Add vanilla and mix until batter is smooth. Spoon batter onto sauce in DO-do not mix or smooth out batter. Bake 40-50 minutes, or until cake is puffed and golden and knife inserted into cake comes out clean. Serve directly from DO, spooning caramel sauce over individual servings, and top with whipped cream.

Before Trip:

- Make cranberry sauce. Put in MSB and refrigerate.
- Buy skinless chicken breasts. Put in ZLB and freeze.
- Mix glaze for chicken. Put in MSB and put in refrigerator until trip. This does not have to be kept in the cooler.
- Make beet and Roquefort salad according to recipe.
- Buy Lipton Noodles and Sauce. Consult back of package as to what ingredients to bring on trip. Put in ZLB.
- For Chomeur, put dry ingredients in a ZLB. Butter can also be put in a ZLB.
- You can use powdered milk or buy a small carton of milk. Keep upright in your cooler. Take a small plastic container to store your vanilla. Don't forget your egg.

On Trip:

- Set out crackers, cheese, and cranberry sauce (in a bowl with a spoon).
- Make sure your chicken is thawed out the day before your dinner.
- Get coals hot for 2 DOs.
- Pour beet salad into serving dish.
- Put chicken with glaze on top in DO and bake.
- Make Chomeur. Put in DO and bake.
- About 15 minutes before chicken is finished baking make your Lipton Noodle dish.
- Set everything out to be served except your Chomeur which should still be baking. If it has finished baking set it aside until you are ready to serve it after dinner.
- Do not forget your wine. After all, you do not want anyone to get upset.

Menu Seven

Days 1 - 4

Breakfast

Texas Egg Casserole

Fruit Salad

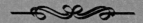

Lunch

Black Bean Hummus with Salsa and Pita Bread

Pickled Vegetables

Pepperidge Farm Cookies

Dinner

Spicy Peanut Dip

Indian Chicken

Rice Pilaf with Cinnamon and Shallot Butter

Cucumber Raita

Cashew Nut Fudge

Spiced Hot Tea

Texas Egg Casserole

Serves 14.

6 slices white or wheat bread, crust removed
1 lb ground sausage; I use Italian
2 small onions, chopped
1 4-oz. can of chopped green chiles
1 jalapeno, chopped
4 cups shredded cheddar cheese
6 eggs
1 t salt
1 t dry mustard or 2 t Dijon mustard
2 cups of half and half, or milk
1 t seasoned salt
1 t ground cumin

Lightly butter each slice of bread. Place bread in a 12-inch buttered DO. Brown sausage with chopped onions. Sprinkle drained green chiles and jalapeno over sausage and put in DO on bread. Sprinkle with grated cheese. In a bowl, beat eggs, add seasoned salt, ground cumin, mustard, and milk or half and half. Mix well. Pour over all. Bake on coals for 35-45 minutes or until casserole is bubbly and lightly browned on top. This casserole is best when it stands 30 minutes after baking, but it is not essential.

Fruit Salad

Serves 8.

This can be any combination of fresh fruits at your grocery store. I like to buy fruit that is in season because it usually lasts for a longer time and has a better flavor. I allow 3/4-1 cup fruit per person.

One of my all time favorite combinations of fruit consists of mangos and strawberries. You will need 4 large mangos and 2 pints of strawberries. Remember that mangos have a large seed in the center. Peel the mango with a sharp knife. Starting at either end of the mango, slice into sections (like an orange) all the way to the seed. Take out one section to get it started, then cut along each other section to help remove the flesh from the seed. Your strawberries should already be washed and hulled. Slice them in half and arrange them on a serving dish with your mango. Or mix them together in a large bowl. Sometimes I add kiwi for a different texture and color. This dish not only looks good, but tastes good.

Before Trip:

- Buy bread, remove crusts for 6 slices, put in ZLB and label.
- Brown sausage and onions, add green chiles, jalapeno, and other spices. Put in ZLB/MSB, and freeze until trip.
- Put cheese in ZLB in refrigerator.
- The day before trip, break eggs into a plastic bottle with a wide opening. Make sure the lid is on tight. Keep refrigerated.
- Buy fresh fruit the day before your trip. Make sure your strawberries are dry, pat dry with a paper towel if necessary. Put in a ZLB with a dry paper towel. Keep refrigerated. The mangos do not have to be kept refrigerated. Neither do kiwi if they are not quite ripe.

On Trip:

- Prepare coals for egg casserole.
- Make casserole according to recipe.
- While casserole is baking, make your fruit salad.

Black Bean Hummus
with Salsa and Pita Bread

Serves 8.

1/2 lb dried black beans, soaked overnight, drained, and cooked until tender according to package directions, or you can use canned black beans, drained
3/4 lb dried garbanzo beans, soaked overnight, drained, and cooked until tender, or use canned garbanzos, drained
1/2 lb tahini (sesame paste)
2 T minced garlic
juice of 1 or 2 lemons
1/2 cup warm water
1/2 cup good quality olive oil
3 t ground cumin
salt and pepper, to taste

1 jar of salsa
1 15-oz. can sliced olives

Puree all ingredients in a food processor or blender until a fine consistency is achieved. Taste and correct seasoning if necessary. Seal in an MSB, label, and refrigerate until trip. This will keep up to 2 weeks.

For the salsa you can buy it (one 16-oz. jar) already made or you can make your own. Refer to Days 1-4, Menu 3 for a great salsa recipe. Split your pita bread and fill with generous amounts of hummus, salsa, and olives.

Pickled Vegetables

Serves 8.
You can buy pickled vegetables (one 16-oz. jar) at the grocery store. Some of them are very tasty. Or you can use the following marinated vegetable recipe.

Vegetables: 3/4 lb cut green beans, or a mixture of green and wax beans, blanched
1 small onion, preferably red, thinly sliced
1/4 lb zucchini, sliced lengthwise into quarters, blanched
1/2 lb slender carrot sticks or whole baby carrots, blanched
1/4 lb halved fresh mushrooms

Marinade: 1/2 cup olive oil
1/4 cup herb vinegar
1/4 t tarragon, crushed
1/4 t chervil, crushed
pinch of cayenne pepper
salt and fresh ground black pepper
1 clove garlic

After you have prepared your vegetables, whip all marinade ingredients in a blender for a few seconds. Pour marinade over cooled vegetables and toss. This needs to be made at least a day in advance, but once made it will last up to 2 weeks in the refrigerator. Be careful not to overcook your vegetables. Sometimes I use green onions or leeks. Be experimental and try all sorts of vegetables. Put in MSB with some of the marinade until your trip.

Before Trip:

- Make hummus. Store in refrigerator in plastic container, ZLB/MSB.
- Put pita bread in a ZLB.
- Put salsa in a plastic container.
- Make or buy pickled vegetables and put in plastic container, ZLB/MSB.
- Buy Pepperidge Farm cookies (3 per person is usually enough).

On Trip:

- Set out hummus, salsa, olives, pita bread, pickled vegetables, and cookies. Let everyone help themselves.

Spicy Peanut Dip

Serves 6-8.

> 1 piece fresh ginger, 1 x 1 x 1 inch, peeled
> 3 large garlic cloves, peeled
> 2 cups unsalted dry roasted peanuts
> 3 T all-purpose soy sauce
> 1 1/2 T sugar
> 2 T Chinese rice wine
> 1 1/2 T Chinese black vinegar, preferably Chinkiang
> 1/4 cup oriental sesame oil
> 1 t hot chili paste
> 1/4 cup chicken stock
> 1 T finely chopped scallion greens, for garnish (opt.)

You can make this recipe in a blender or a food processor. Drop the ginger and garlic through the feed tube of a food processor with the metal blade in place and the motor running. Process until finely chopped, about 20 seconds. Reserve. Process 1 1/3 cups of the peanuts until smooth, about 3 minutes. Add the remaining 2/3 cup peanuts and the ginger-garlic mixture and remaining ingredients, except the scallion greens, and process until combined, about 15 seconds. Store in a plastic container in refrigerator until your trip. This will keep 2-3 weeks in your cooler.

Use any of your favorite vegetables. Vegetables I recommend for this dip are:

> 4 oz. of snow peas, blanched
> 2 medium red peppers, stem, core, and seeds removed
> 2 medium yellow peppers, stem, core, and seeds removed
> 3-4 large carrots, peeled and sliced
> 1 medium cucumber, peeled and seeded

Place in a serving dish and garnish the dip with the scallion greens. Put the dish in the center of a vegetable platter and serve.

Indian Chicken

Serves 8.

3 lbs boneless, skinless chicken breasts
4 garlic cloves, peeled
1-inch piece fresh ginger root, peeled and halved
16-oz. can stewed or plain tomatoes
4 T tomato paste
2 T ground coriander

2 T fennel seed
2 t ground cumin
2 t turmeric
1 t salt
1/2 t ground cinnamon

I make this recipe in a food processor for quickness, but you can do everything manually if you do not have a processor. Slice the chicken into 1/4-inch strips. Transfer to a 3-quart mixing bowl and set aside. Use the metal blade and, with the machine running, drop the garlic and ginger through the feed tube and process until minced. Stop the machine, add the remaining ingredients and process for 30 seconds, stopping once to scrape down the bowl. Add to the sliced chicken and stir together gently to coat the chicken with marinade. Refrigerate, covered, for at least 6 hours or preferable overnight. Put in MSB, label, and freeze until your trip. To cook this you will need a 12-inch DO set on your grill over coals. If you have ever done a Chinese stir fry your skills will come in handy. Let your DO heat up for a few minutes on the grill. With tongs or a spoon try to get as much chicken out of your bags as possible, without the marinade sauce, and put in your DO. Stir chicken until it is slightly cooked, then add the marinade sauce and simmer for about 20 minutes, or until chicken is cooked, with the lid off. This is an easy dish with wonderful flavors.

Rice Pilaf with Cinnamon and Shallot Butter

Serves 8.
This is an unusual spiced pilaf, and oh so yummy.

3 medium shallots, peeled
1 stick unsalted butter, at room temperature
1/2 t ground cinnamon
pinch ground cloves
1/2 t salt

1/4 t fresh ground black pepper
1 1/2 cups uncooked rice, I use Basmati or Jasmine
1 small piece stick cinnamon
1 1/2 cups chicken stock
1 1/2 cups water

Once again I use my food processor for ease. Process the shallots with the metal blade of a food processor until coarsely chopped, about 5 pulses. Rinse under running water and squeeze dry with paper towels to remove any bitter juices. Process all but 1 T of the stick of butter, the shallots, ground cinnamon, cloves, salt and pepper until blended; pulse 3 times, then scrape the side of the work bowl and pulse 4 more times. The shallots should still be in pieces. Transfer to a small bowl, cover and set aside for a least 2 hours so flavors have a chance to blend. To make the pilaf, melt the remaining 1 T of butter in a medium saucepan. Stir in the rice and toss to coat with the butter. Add the cinnamon stick, stock, and water and bring to a boil. Reduce the heat, cover, and simmer until the liquid has been absorbed and the rice is just tender, about 17 minutes. Stir in the shallot butter. Toss gently and season to taste. Put in MSB/ZLB, and freeze until trip. This will freeze well for 1-2 months.

Cucumber Raita

Serves 6.
This is a nice cool dish to accompany the more spicy foods.

> 1 large cucumber
> 2 cups plain yogurt, White Mountain Bulgarian yogurt is my favorite
> 2 T chopped cilantro (fresh coriander) or parsley
> 2 T chopped fresh mint
> 1 jalapeno pepper, seeded, finely chopped
> salt to taste
> 1 t cumin seeds or 1/2 t ground cumin
> 2 t mustard seeds or 1 t dry mustard

At home before your trip, put cumin seeds and mustard seeds in a skillet and dry roast over medium heat 1 to 2 minutes, until they begin to pop. Cool, put in a ZLB. Or you can put the ground cumin and dry mustard in a ZLB, your choice. On your trip, cut cucumber into matchstick-size pieces, I leave out the seeds, and place in a bowl. Add yogurt, cilantro, mint, chile, salt, and your bag of spices. Stir gently to mix. Keep in cooler until ready to serve.

Cashew Nut Fudge

Serves 6. Each person gets 2 pieces of fudge.

This is a good way to end an Indian meal because it is light, easy, and goes well with the spiced tea. This recipe will keep in the freezer up to 2-3 months. It will also keep in the refrigerator for 3-4 weeks. Make sure it is well wrapped and kept in a dry, semi-cool place on your boat.

> 3/4 cup unsalted cashew nuts, if you cannot find unsalted
> cashews, rinse the salted nuts under water to remove the salt
> 3/4 cup boiling water
> 1 T milk
>
> 1/3 cup sugar
> 1/2 T butter
> 1/2 t vanilla

Put cashew nuts in a bowl, top with boiling water and soak 1 hour. Grease and line a 4-inch square pan with waxed paper. Drain cashew nuts thoroughly and put in a blender or food processor fitted with the metal blade. Add milk and process until smooth, scraping mixture down from side once or twice. Stir in sugar. Heat a large non-stick skillet, add butter and melt over medium-low heat. Add nut paste and cook about 20 minutes, stirring constantly, until mixture is very thick. Be sure to scrape bottom of pan while cooking to get the caramelized bits. Sir in vanilla, then spoon into prepared pan and spread evenly. Cool completely, then cut fudge into about 12 diamond shaped pieces using a wet sharp knife. Store in a ZLB or plastic container until trip. These are fragile so one has to be careful cutting, removing from pan, and storing.

Spiced Hot Tea

Makes 3 small pots, about 8-10 cups of tea.

3/10 t black peppercorns	1 t ground ginger
3/16 t cardamom seeds	hot tea
3/16 t whole cloves	boiling water
1/4-inch cinnamon stick	milk and sugar to taste

Put peppercorns, cardamom seeds, cloves and cinnamon in a mortar and grind to a fine powder with a pestle. Add ginger and grind again a few seconds to mix. Add about 1/2 t of spice mixture to a pot of tea; leave in a warm place 1 to 2 minutes to brew. Serve hot, with milk and sugar. Store spice mixture in an airtight container, in a dark cupboard to preserve its flavor. For your raft trip put it in a ZLB. This will keep 2 to 3 months.

Before Trip:

- Make spicy peanut dip. Prepare all vegetables, except cucumber, and put in ZLB the day before your trip. To keep your carrots really crisp and crunchy put them in MSB with some water. You can always use carrot water for other things. Remember, waste not, want not. Who said that anyway?
- Make the Indian chicken.
- Make the rice dish.
- For the cucumber dish, put whole cucumbers in a ZLB. Make sure your yogurt containers are plastic. Wash and dry your fresh herbs and put in a ZLB with a paper towel. Put your jalapeno pepper in a ZLB. Remember to take your ZLB of spices.
- Make cashew nut fudge.
- Make spiced tea mixture. Put loose tea leaves or tea bags in a ZLB. Put sugar in a ZLB.

On Trip:

- Make sure everything is thawed out the night before you prepare your dinner. It is not much fun sitting around waiting for your food to thaw out. Or trying to thaw it out by burning it and then having to make up excuses about what happened.
- Set out the peanut dip and vegetables and let people get started eating.
- Get your coals ready for the Indian chicken.
- Empty your rice into a pan on your stove and start it on low heat.
- Make your cucumber dish.
- Start chicken cooking.
- Put water on for tea.
- When chicken is ready, set out with the rice and cucumber.
- When you are finished being a glutton, make the tea and set out the cashew nut fudge. Remember the sugar and milk for the tea.

Menu Eight

Days 1 - 4

Breakfast

Almond French Toast

Turkey Bacon

Lunch

Chicken Salad Sandwiches with Mango Chutney

Carrot Sticks

Fresh Cherries and Grapes

Spice Cookies

Dinner

Stuffed Cucumbers with Smoked Salmon

Creamy Pasta with Fresh Herbs

Mixed Vegetable and Pine Nut Salad

Fresh Baked Bread

Chocolate Chocolate Brownies

Strawberries Marinated in Grand Marnier

Chardonnay or Chenin Blanc

Almond French Toast

Serves 8.

This recipe is also good with a tangy orange marmalade or yogurt. It is delicious, too, with sliced apples or pears, sautéed in butter and sugar, or maple syrup, until slightly caramelized.

16 slices sourdough, French, or homemade white bread,
about 4 inches square and 3/8 inch thick
6 oz. commercial almond paste, or use recipe that follows
4 oz. cream cheese
8 large eggs

1 cup milk
1 t vanilla
6 T butter
2 T vegetable oil

I use a food processor for this recipe. Trim crusts from bread. Use metal blade to process the crusts until very fine. Set aside in a shallow dish. Process almond paste and cream cheese with metal blade until smooth, scraping down the side of the bowl as necessary. Set aside. Put eggs, milk and vanilla in bowl, and process just until mixed. (This makes about 2 2/3 cups.) Pour into a shallow dish. Make 8 sandwiches using the almond mixture as filling, be generous. Slice each diagonally to form two triangles. Dip the triangles on both sides in the egg mixture, then in the crumbs, then again in the egg mixture. To freeze put a piece of wax paper on a cookie sheet and place the triangles of bread on wax paper and put in freezer for a few hours, until hard. Then put them in a ZLB, label and put back in freezer. I like to make these for small groups, 6-8 people, because they do require a little more room in your cooler. They are worth finding room for since they are simply scrumptious. Make sure they are thawed out before you begin to cook them. Heat oil and butter in a large skillet over medium-high heat. Cook the triangles for about 3 minutes on each side or until golden brown. Serve with maple syrup.

Almond Paste

2 cups (1/2 lb) blanched almonds
1 cup confectioners sugar
4 T (1/2 stick) butter

2 egg whites
1/2 t almond extract

Use metal blade to process the almonds and sugar together for 2 minutes, scraping down side of bowl as necessary. Add butter and process 30 seconds. Add egg whites and almond extract and process for 1 minute more. Store in a tightly covered jar in refrigerator or freezer. Almond paste will keep in refrigerator for a month, or in freezer indefinitely. Makes about 16 ounces.

Before Trip:

- Make almond French toast.
- Put maple syrup in a plastic container.
- Buy and freeze turkey bacon. It will last longer in your cooler if you start out with it frozen. Or you can buy bacon, fully cooked ready to serve, in a box. Yep, isn't it amazing? All you have to do is heat it up in a skillet. And it does not have to be refrigerated.

On Trip:

- Be sure your French toast and turkey bacon are thawed out the night before you are preparing your fabulous breakfast.
- Start frying or heating your bacon in a skillet on your stove. Fry most of it and keep it in foil next to your burner so it will keep warm.
- Set out the maple syrup.
- Cook the French toast, serve, and listen for the sounds of contentment among your rafting buddies.

Chicken Salad Sandwiches
with Mango Chutney

Serves 6-8.

4 cups cooked, shredded chicken breast
2 cups chopped celery
3/4 cup sliced, drained, canned water chestnuts
1/2 cup mayonnaise
1/2 cup yogurt or sour cream
1 t salt (opt.)
1 8-oz. jar Major Grey Mango Chutney
1 cup dry roasted peanuts
2 cups fresh alfalfa sprouts (hippie hair as we call it)
12-16 slices of sourdough bread or bread of your choice

I make this recipe up the day before I leave and put it in a ZLB in the refrigerator. Mix the mayonnaise and yogurt together at home and store in a plastic container, as long as you keep it cold at all times. This is to be added a few hours before you make your sandwiches. If you choose to make this salad on the river it is best to cook and shred your chicken breasts at home, put in a ZLB, and freeze. You could also cut up the rest of the ingredients and put them in a ZLB and mix them with the chicken on the river trip. Combine all the ingredients with the exception of the peanuts. These should be added right before you make your sandwiches. Put your chicken salad on your bread with some hippie hair and think what a wonderful rafting experience.

Carrot Sticks

See Days 1-4, Menu 6.
It is always nice to have fresh carrot sticks.

Spice Cookies

Makes about 4 dozen cookies.

1/2 cup pistachios or other nuts of your choice
2 cups white flour
1 t baking powder
1/8 t salt
1/2 t cinnamon
1/8 t nutmeg
1/8 t white pepper
dash ground cloves

1/4 t anise seed
1/2 cup sugar
3 pieces lemon rind removed with a vegetable peeler
3/4 stick unsalted butter, cut into 6 equal pats
1 large egg
1 t fresh lemon juice
1/2 cup confectioners sugar
1 T water

I use my food processor for this recipe but you can also do it manually. Use the metal blade of a food processor to chop the pistachios finely, about 10 seconds. Remove and reserve about one-third of the chopped nuts. Add the next 8 ingredients to the remaining nuts in the work bowl. Pulse 2 to 4 times to combine. Reserve. Process the sugar and lemon rind for 1 minute or until the rind is finely chopped. Add the butter and process until smooth and creamy, about 20 seconds, stopping to scrape down the work bowl as necessary. Add the egg and lemon juice and process for 5 seconds. Add the reserved dry ingredients and pulse 8 to 10 times or until well mixed, stopping to scrape down the bowl as necessary. Wrap the dough well in plastic wrap and refrigerate overnight. Preheat the oven to 350°. Roll about 1 heaping teaspoon of dough at a time into a ball. Place about 1 1/2 inches apart on lightly greased baking sheets. Bake the cookies in the center of the oven until firm but not brown, 10 to 12 minutes. Place on wire rack to cool. Stir together the confectioners sugar and the water. Dip the top of each cookie in the glaze and sprinkle with the reserved chopped pistachio nuts. Put in a ZLB and freeze until your trip. These can be frozen up to 1 month. The spicy flavor in these cookies is delicious.

Before Trip:

- Do carrot sticks the day before your trip.
- Wash and dry grapes and cherries, put in a ZLB with paper towel the day before your trip. Keep refrigerated.
- Make spice cookies.

On Trip:

- Set out the chicken salad after you have added the mayonnaise, yogurt, and peanuts. Set out the hippie hair and bread.
- Drain water or marinade off carrots and set out.
- Set out cherries, grapes, or other fresh fruit.
- Set out spice cookies.
- EAT!

Stuffed Cucumbers
with Smoked Salmon

Serves 6.

2 medium cucumbers, cut length wise, peeled and seeds removed
1/2 lb smoked salmon (dry, not lox)
1/4 to 1/2 cup yogurt, mayonnaise, or sour cream (opt.)
fresh dill or 3 t dried dill

When I make this I leave out the yogurt because I enjoy the flavor of just the smoked salmon and dill. Some people prefer a little moisture so you might want to add the yogurt. After you have prepared the cucumbers, slice them into 1 1/2 inch pieces. Crumble up your salmon (mix in your yogurt) and stuff your hollowed out pieces of cucumber with it. As a last touch put a sprig of fresh dill on top as a garnish or sprinkle a little dried dill on top.

Creamy Pasta with Fresh Herbs

Serves 6.

1 1/2 cups heavy cream, I prefer half and half
4 T sweet butter
1/2 t salt
1/8 t nutmeg
pinch of cayenne

1/4 cup grated imported Parmesan cheese
1 cup finely chopped mixed fresh herbs; parsley, mint, basil, chives, salad burnet, and watercress (this one you might find on one of your raft trips)
1 lb angel hair pasta or other thin pasta

Combine first 5 ingredients in a heavy saucepan and simmer for 15 minutes, or until sauce is slightly reduced and thickened. Whisk in Parmesan and fresh herbs, and simmer for another 5 minutes. Taste and correct seasoning. Serve immediately. Light and simple

Mixed Vegetable and Pine Nut Salad

Serves 6.

1 head of lettuce, I use red leaf lettuce, washed and torn into bite sized pieces
2 medium zucchini, sliced 1/4 inch thick and blanched
one bunch of radishes, usually 8-10, washed and sliced
1 small jar of pickled baby corn, drained and rinsed in water
1/4 cup roasted pine nuts or other nuts
4 oz. of blue cheese
1 bottle Italian dressing transferred to a plastic container

Mix all ingredients together and let everyone add their own amount of dressing.

Fresh Baked Bread

See Days 1-4, Menu 1.

Chocolate Chocolate Brownies

You have several choices here. You can be lazy and take the easy way out and use a box brownie mix (Ghirardelli is the best) on your raft trip, prepared in your DO. Or you can make the recipe below ahead of time and freeze in a ZLB. But if you are a real gourmet and want people to smack their lips with utter delight, you will make the following recipe on your trip in a DO with no complaints.

Makes 16 2-inch squares.

3/4 cup flour	6 oz. (1 cup) bittersweet chocolate chips (Callebault or Ghirardelli)
1/4 t baking soda	1 t vanilla
1/4 t salt	2 eggs
5 1/2 T butter	3/4 cup chopped pecans or walnuts
3/4 cup sugar	1 cup semi-sweet chocolate chips
2 T water	

Keep your chocolate chips in the cooler on your trip. In small bowl, combine flour, baking soda and salt. In sauce pan, bring butter, sugar, and water to a boil. Immediately remove from heat. Add 1 cup bittersweet chocolate chips and vanilla, stirring until chips are melted and mixture is smooth. Transfer mixture to large bowl. Add eggs, one at a time, beating well after each addition. Gradually blend in flour mixture. Stir in nuts and semi-sweet chocolate chips. Spread into a greased 10-inch DO. Bake 30-40 minutes until you smell that wonderful aroma. It is easy to cut these if they are cooled completely if you can possibly wait. If you make these at home, bake at 325° for 30-35 minutes. Mmmmm, good!

Strawberries Marinated in Grand Marnier

Serves 6.

Do this right before you start preparing dinner. Put strawberries (about 2 cups) in a bowl and drizzle 1/4 cup Grand Marnier on top, cover and set aside until dessert time. To get really decadent you might want to try a liqueur called Mandarine Napoleon. Either way you cannot go wrong.

Before Trip:

- Put cucumbers in ZLB.
- Put smoked salmon in ZLB.
- Put dill in ZLB.
- Put cream in MSB.
- Put butter in ZLB.
- Measure spices for pasta and put together in ZLB.
- Wash, dry, and put fresh herbs in ZLB.
- Put grated Parmesan cheese in ZLB.
- Put uncooked pasta in ZLB.
- Wash and dry lettuce the day before trip. Put in a ZLB with 1 or 2 paper towels, squeeze out air and close bag.
- Wash and dry zucchini and put in ZLB.
- Wash and dry radishes and put in ZLB.
- Transfer pickled baby corn with some of its juice to a plastic container or MSB.
- Roast pine nuts in a toaster oven or regular oven until slightly brown, 350°, cool, put in a ZLB.
- Put blue cheese in ZLB.
- Do not forget your Italian dressing.
- Put white wine in a plastic bottle.
- Put bread in ZLB.
- Put chocolate chips in ZLB.
- Put chocolate chips and nuts in ZLB.
- Measure out flour, baking soda, and salt for brownies and put in ZLB.
- Put butter in ZLB.
- Put sugar in ZLB.
- Make sure vanilla is in a plastic container.
- Put strawberries in a ZLB with a paper towel.
- Put your Grand Marnier in a plastic container. Perhaps you may want to add a little extra for late night sipping.

On Trip:

- Prepare cucumbers and smoked salmon so people can munch down while you cook dinner.
- Start coals for baking bread and brownies. Grease 2 DOs.
- Make the mixed vegetable salad.
- Make brownies, put in DO on coals.
- Put bread in DO on coals.
- Marinate strawberries in Grand Marnier.
- Make pasta. Remember to boil pasta about 10 minutes before the bread is finished baking.
- Do not forget about your brownies.
- Serve the pasta from the stove so that it does not get cold. Set everything out buffet style.
- Set out the desserts when everyone has finished with dinner and let the hawgs run wild!

Menu Nine
Days 1 - 4

Breakfast
Tofu Scrambler

Prune Bran Muffins with Fruit Preserves

Honeydew Melon

Lunch
Couscous Salad

Assortment of Crackers

Big Red Apples

Lindt Chocolate Bars

Dinner
Sham Boursin au Poivre

Potatoes Moussaka

Nutted Wild Rice

Crescent Dinner Rolls

Grand Marnier Cake

Sauvignon Blanc

Tofu Scrambler

Serves 8.

2 t canola oil
1 cup chopped green onion
1 red pepper, diced
12 mushrooms, chopped
2 lbs tofu, drained and mashed with a fork
2 T mirin (a Japanese style sweetened sake found in most grocery stores)
2 T tamari
2 t dried basil
1 t granulated garlic (opt.)
1 t curry powder
fresh ground pepper to taste

Sauté first 3 ingredients in oil for 3 minutes. Add rest of ingredients and cook for five minutes, stirring frequently. Adjust seasonings to taste.

Prune Bran Muffins with Fruit Preserves

Makes 16-18 muffins. I allow 2 muffins per person.
This recipe is always a mover, need I say more?

1 cup bran buds or other bran cereal
1 1/4 cup flour
12 pitted prunes (4 oz.) or other dried fruit, coarsely chopped
1 t baking soda
1 t salt

1 large egg
2/3 cup sugar
1 t baking powder
1/2 cup vegetable oil
1 1/4 cups buttermilk or milk
1 1/2 t vanilla

Spray or grease a 12-inch DO. Make sure your coals are ready. Mix the first 6 ingredients. Beat egg and sugar, pour in oil, and mix. Add buttermilk and vanilla and continue to mix. Add dry ingredients and blend just until the flour disappears. Pour into greased DO and bake 20 to 25 minutes, until the muffins are a golden color. Remove from the fire, cut into squares, and serve with your favorite fruit preserves.

Before Trip:

- Put oil in a plastic container.
- Wash green onions, red pepper, and mushrooms. Put in ZLB and keep refrigerated.
- Put tofu in a ZLB.
- Put spices in a ZLB.
- Put tamari and mirin in a MSB or plastic container.
- Put first 6 ingredients for muffins in ZLB.
- Put sugar in ZLB.
- You can use powdered eggs or you can find a safe place in your cooler for your eggs. Refer to front of book on eggs.
- Buttermilk also comes in powder form these days, check into it. I use a product called SACO cultured buttermilk blend found in the baking section at the grocery store. Or use powdered milk. Put in a ZLB.
- Put your vanilla in a plastic container.
- Buy honeydew melon. Allow 1 melon for 4 to 5 people.

On Trip:

- Get coals ready for muffins.
- Slice melon.
- Make prune bran muffins and start baking ASAP.
- Get everything ready to cook tofu. Start cooking when muffins are 5 minutes from being done. Set everything out and go for it!

Couscous Salad

Serves 6 (about 6 oz. each).

1 1/2 cups couscous
1/2 cup loosely packed parsley leaves, finely chopped
1 medium cucumber, seeded, peeled, and coarsely chopped
3 medium tomatoes, seeded, and coarsely chopped
6 medium scallions, trimmed and thinly sliced
1/4 cup pine nuts, toasted

Cook the couscous according to the package directions. Set aside. For quickness I do the salad in a food processor 2-3 days before I plan on serving the salad. Process the parsley with the metal blade of a food processor until finely chopped, about 10 seconds; reserve. Coarsely chop the cucumber, about 6 pulses; reserve. Coarsely chop the tomatoes, 4 to 6 pulses; reserve. Process the scallions with the thin slicing disc. Combine all the ingredients and toss with the Mustard Vinaigrette (can be done day before if desired).

Mustard Vinaigrette

1 t coarse salt
1/2 t ground pepper
2 T red wine vinegar

1 1/2 t Dijon mustard
1/2 cup olive oil

Process all ingredients with the metal blade until combined. Or put all ingredients in a jar and shake the heck out of it. Adjust the seasoning. If you want some variation, substitute 1 T chopped fresh tarragon, or 1 t dried, for mustard in the recipe above. Put in a ZLB and refrigerate.

Before Trip:

- Make couscous salad. This can be made on your trip but be sure vegetables are washed, and put ingredients in ZLB.
- Make salad dressing. Put in a plastic container.
- I usually allow 6-10 small crackers per person. If I have lots of room I keep the crackers in their boxes so as not to crush them. Nothing like serving crumbs to your buddies. You can count on someone who will make a "smart" remark.
- Wash your apples and find a protective, cool place to store them until you devour them.
- I usually hide my chocolate bars in the cooler, in a disguised water proof bag, for fear of them being consumed before I want them to be.

On Trip:

- Set out salad, add dressing.
- Set out crackers, apples, and bring out chocolate bars for the grand finale.

Sham Boursin au Poivre

Serves 6-8.

> 16 oz. cream cheese
> 2 cloves of garlic, minced
> 2 t basil
> 2 t dill weed
> 2 t chopped chives, dried
> lemon pepper

Blend first 5 ingredients. Pat into round flat shape. Roll generously in lemon pepper on all sides. Make a few days ahead. Put in a ZLB and keep refrigerated. Serve with crackers. This spread gets instant raves.

Potatoes Moussaka

Serves 8.

This recipe is best made on your river trip.

> 2 lbs red potatoes, thinly sliced (about 6 medium)
> 3/4 t salt
> 1/4 cup (4 T) butter or margarine, divided
> 1 large onion, chopped
> 3 cloves of garlic, minced
> 1 small eggplant, peeled and cubed
> 1 cup chopped tomato
> 1/2 t dried basil
> 1/2 t dried oregano
> 1/2 t ground cinnamon
> 2 T flour
> 2 cups milk
> 1/2 cup grated good Parmesan cheese

Layer potatoes in a 12-inch DO; sprinkle with salt, and set aside. Melt 2 T butter in a large skillet; add onion and garlic. Cook over medium heat, stirring constantly, 5 minutes. Add eggplant and next 4 ingredients; cook 5 minutes, stirring often. Spoon mixture over potatoes. Melt remaining 2 T butter in a saucepan over low heat; add flour, stirring until smooth. At this point you may want to use a whisk. Cook 1 minute, stirring constantly. Gradually add milk; cook over medium heat, stirring constantly, until mixture is thickened and bubbly. Pour over eggplant mixture; sprinkle with Parmesan cheese. Bake for 35 to 40 minutes or until potatoes are tender. This is a great tasting vegetarian dish that all will enjoy.

Nutted Wild Rice

Serves 6.
I love the hint of citrus flavor and different textures in this rice recipe. It is gooood, I will tell you to your face it is gooood!

1 cup raw wild rice, from Minnesota
5 1/2 cups defatted chicken stock, or water, or you can cheat like I do sometimes when in a hurry and use chicken bouillon cubes or chicken broth in a can or box
1 cup shelled pecans
1 cup yellow or other raisins
grated rind of 1 large orange
1/2 cup chopped fresh mint
4 green onions, thinly sliced
1/4 cup olive oil
1/3 cup fresh orange juice
1 1/2 t salt
ground pepper, to taste

Put rice in a strainer and run under cold water; rinse thoroughly. Add stock or water and bring to a rapid boil. Adjust heat to a gentle simmer and cook uncovered for 45 minutes. After 30 minutes check for doneness; rice should not be too soft. Place a thin towel inside a colander and turn rice into the colander and drain. Transfer drained rice to a bowl. Add remaining ingredients to rice and toss gently. Adjust seasonings to taste. Let mixture stand at least 2 hours to allow flavors to develop. Can be served at room temperature. This will last 6 to 8 days in the refrigerator. Put in a ZLB.

Crescent Dinner Rolls

Makes 18 small rolls.

Go to the store and buy two 8-oz. cans of Pillsbury Crescent Dinner Rolls. Keep refrigerated and in ZLB until you are ready to prepare them. Follow instructions on side of can. Next place rolls in lightly greased DO and bake until lightly brown and you can smell the wonderful aroma. Be sure and check them after about 10 minutes so they will not burn.

Grand Marnier Cake

Serves 12-14.

This is probably my second most favorite cake, the first being a two orgasmic chocolate cake. This cake literally melts in your mouth. This should be made in camp if you have the time. It is well worth the effort and will guarantee you friends for life.

2 cups sugar	1 cup sour cream
1 cup butter	1 t vanilla
2 eggs	1 T Grand Marnier or orange juice for the wimps
2 cups flour, not sifted	1 cup coarsely ground pecans
1/2 t salt	grated rind of 1 orange
1 t baking powder	

Topping:　　　4 T butter, melted　　　　　　1/3 cup Grand Marnier

Put flour, salt, and baking powder in a ZLB before your trip. Cream sugar and butter thoroughly and blend in eggs. Add dry ingredients to butter mixture alternately with the sour cream, vanilla, and Grand Marnier or orange juice. Blend in pecans and orange rind. Pour into a well buttered and floured 12-inch DO. Bake 1 hour to 1 hour and 20 minutes. Stick a toothpick in the cake and if it comes out clean it is finished baking. Take the DO off the coals and let cool while you make the topping. Melt the butter and add the Grand Marnier. Pierce the entire top of the cake and pour mixture over. Cool for 30 minutes (if you can wait that long) in the pan. And dig in!

Before Trip: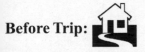

- Make Sham Boursin au Poivre.
- Don't forget the potatoes.
- Put butter in ZLB.
- The day before your trip, chop up onion and garlic, put in ZLB.
- Put the eggplant in an open plastic bag in a cool place until ready to use. Eggplants usually last up to 1 week on a raft trip.
- Wash tomato.
- Combine spices, put in ZLB.
- You can use carton milk. I prefer to use powdered milk because it is easier to deal with and you can put it in, what else, a ZLB.
- Make nutted wild rice a few days before trip.
- Put Pillsbury cans in a ZLB and keep refrigerated.
- Measure and put all dry ingredients for cake in ZLB, including powdered eggs if using.
- Add vanilla to sour cream container, put in ZLB.
- Measure amount of Grand Marnier needed and put in plastic container.
- Put ground pecans in ZLB.
- Be sure you have 3 DOs for this meal.

On Trip: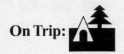

- Make enough coals for potato dish, rolls, and cake.
- Set out some of the wine and boursin and let people begin to nibble.
- Make potato moussaka.
- Make Grand Marnier cake and start baking.
- Put nutted wild rice in a serving dish.
- Bake rolls when moussaka is about 10 minutes from being done.
- Serve your dinner. And when your fabulous cake is finished baking blow the trumpets!

Menu Ten

Days 1 - 4

Breakfast

Banana-Nut Waffles

Fresh Berries with Creme Fraiche

Lunch

Pissaladiere Sandwiches

Olive Nut Spread

Grapes and Nectarines

Vanilla Sand Cookies

Dinner

Brie Pinwheel

Sweet-Sour Beef Kabobs

Spinach with Red Onion and Walnuts

Peppered Buttered Flat Noodles

Orange Wine Cake

Zinfandel

Banana-Nut Waffles

Makes 4-5 waffles.
These waffles are very good. They do require some room in your cooler. It is definitely worth the space to have homemade waffles on a raft trip.

2 cups sifted all-purpose flour
3 t baking powder
1/4 t salt
1/8 t nutmeg
3 eggs, separated
1 1/2 cups milk

6 T butter, melted
1 t vanilla
1 T sugar
1 cup mashed ripe bananas (2 to 3 bananas)
1/2 cup chopped nuts (opt.)
maple syrup

Preheat waffle iron. Stir together first 4 ingredients. Beat egg yolks with milk, butter and vanilla. Add to dry ingredients; beat until smooth. Beat egg whites until soft peaks form; gradually beat in sugar and fold into egg yolk mixture with bananas and nuts (if used). Pour batter onto preheated waffle iron and bake according to manufacturer's instructions. Cool and place in ZLB in freezer until trip. Can make 1 month in advance. Serve with maple syrup.

Fresh Berries with Crème Fraiche

Makes 1 cup.

1 cup heavy whipping cream
2 T buttermilk

1-2 qts fresh strawberries, blueberries, or other

Heat cream and buttermilk until lukewarm. Pour into glass jar and cover with plastic wrap or a paper towel. Let sit at room temperature for 24-36 hours, until almost as thick as sour cream. Seal tightly and refrigerate. Will keep for 2-3 weeks. Crème Fraiche is now available in many supermarkets, or you can use drained yogurt.

Before Trip:

- Make waffles and freeze.
- Make or buy Crème Fraiche.
- Put maple syrup in a plastic container in a ZLB.
- Buy berries.

On Trip:

- Heat maple syrup in its container in warm water over a burner on your stove.
- Remove waffles from the cooler and thaw. Heat waffles on a hot griddle with a teaspoon of oil.
- Set out Crème Fraiche and berries and call the cows in for a great breakfast.

Banana Nut Waffles, Page 85

Chama River Campsite, NM   (James Machin)

Pissaladière Sandwiches

Makes 4-6 sandwiches.
This is my version of the pissaladière sauce, which I learned how to make when I cooked in a French restaurant. We used to have our own nickname for it--you don't want to know.

> 4 T olive oil
> 1 can (16-oz.) Italian peeled tomatoes, drained and coarsely chopped
> 2 T tomato paste
> 2 garlic cloves, minced
> 3 T unsalted butter
> 3 medium Spanish onions (about 1 1/2 lbs) peeled and finely chopped
> 3 cans (2-oz.) anchovy fillets, halved lengthwise (opt.)
> 5 small pitted olives, your choice, I like Italian or Greek
> 1/2 cup grated Parmesan cheese
> 1/2 t rosemary, crushed

Heat 2 T of olive oil in a small skillet over moderate heat. Add the tomatoes, tomato paste, and garlic and cook, stirring occasionally, until reduced to a thick puree, about 10 minutes. Set aside. Melt 3 T of the butter in a medium skillet over low heat. Add the onions, cover tightly and cook, stirring once or twice, until the onions are very soft, about 15 minutes. Finely dice the anchovies and halve or quarter the olives. Add these to the onions and cook for 2 to 3 minutes. Add Parmesan cheese and rosemary to the rest of the ingredients and let cool. Put in a ZLB in freezer. Can be made up to 3 or 4 months in advance.

Olive Nut Sread

Makes 3-4 sandwiches.

> 6-oz. cream cheese, softened
> 1/2 cup mayonnaise or drained yogurt
> 1/2 cup chopped pecans
> 1 cup sliced olives, your choice
> 2 T olive juice (use the liquid in the can or bottle)
> Dash of pepper

Mix all the ingredients and let refrigerate for a couple of hours. It will thicken. The olive spread will last up to 2 weeks. I spread this on the bread with the pissaladiere sauce. It makes a wonderful marriage. This can be stored in a ZLB or plastic container.

Vanilla Sand Cookies

Makes 3-4 dozen.

> 3 sticks of butter
> 3 cups flour
> 3/4 cup sugar
> 1 t vanilla (Mexican, if possible)
> 2/3 cup skinless, finely ground almonds

Work all ingredients together with your hands until smooth and stiff. To form the cookies, take a small spoonful or a bit more, and roll into a ball between the palms of your hands. Flatten into a round, and you will have a circle with cracked edges. Arrange on a baking sheet and press a design in the top if you wish. Bake at 325° for about 25 minutes until golden. Cool and store in a ZLB in freezer until your trip. These can be made 1 month in advance. They go great with any type of fruit.

Before Trip: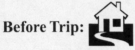

- Make pissaladiere sauce and freeze.
- Make olive nut spread.
- Buy fruit the day before your trip.
- Make cookies.

On Trip:

- Make sandwiches with pissaladiere sauce and olive nut nut spread.
- Set out fruit and cookies. Now sit back and enjoy an easy tasty lunch.

Brie Pinwheel

Serves 6-8.

1 whole Brie, about 1-2 lbs, one that still needs to ripen since it may be
several days before it is consumed

1/2 cup dried currants   1/2 cup finely chopped pecans
1/2 cup chopped fresh dill   1 cup slivered roasted almonds

Carefully cut away the rind from the tip of the Brie. With the back of a knife lightly mark four equal wedge-shaped areas. Sprinkle each wedged area with the above ingredients, patting each garnish into each area. Allow to stand for 20-30 minutes so cheese will soften. Serve with crackers or bread. You can use any combination of ingredients on the Brie.

Sweet-Sour Beef Kabobs

Serves 6.

2 lbs. beef tip, cut into 1-inch cubes   1/4 t pepper
1 beef bouillon cube   1 large bay leaf
1/2 cup hot water   6 whole cloves
1/2 cup brown sugar   1 can (16 oz.) small whole potatoes, drained or 10
3/4 cup cider vinegar   small fresh potatoes (already boiled)
1/2 cup salad oil   16 sweet pickles, cut in half crosswise
1 medium onion, sliced   paprika
2 t salt

Dissolve beef bouillon cube in hot water. In saucepan combine beef bouillon, brown sugar, vinegar, salad oil, onion, salt, pepper, bay leaf and whole cloves. Bring to boil, reduce heat and cook slowly 10 minutes. Cool. Pour marinade over beef cubes and allow to stand in refrigerator for 24 hours, turning occasionally. Put in ZLB and freeze until trip. After thawing beef, remove cubes from marinade and strain and save the marinade. Thread beef cubes alternately with potatoes and pickle halves on 12, (2 skewers, slightly apart, per kabob makes the food stay on better)12-inch skewers. Sprinkle potatoes with paprika. Broil at moderate temperature 3 to 4 inches from heat for a total of 10 to 15 minutes or when done the way you like them. Turn and brush kabobs with marinade frequently.

Spinach with Red Onion and Walnuts

Makes 6 small servings.

1 lb fresh spinach, washed and dried   1/2 cup walnut pieces, toasted
1 large red onion, thinly sliced   poppy seed dressing

Mix the above ingredients and add poppy seed dressing that you purchased at the grocery store. I really like this combination.

Peppered Buttered Flat Noodles

Serves 6-8.

1 16-oz. bag flat noodles   4-6 T butter
Fresh ground black pepper to taste

Follow instructions on package for cooking noodles, drain water off noodles, add butter and black pepper.

Orange Wine Cake

Makes one 9-inch cake.
You can make this with either the orange glaze or wine icing. Can be made in advance or in a DO.

1 medium thick-skinned orange, washed and dried
2 cups flour
1 cup seedless raisins
1 t baking soda
1/2 t salt
1 cup sugar
1/2 cup (1 stick) unsalted butter, at room temperature
2 large eggs
1 cup buttermilk
1 t vanilla
1/2 cup walnuts, finely chopped
orange glaze or wine icing (recipes follow)

With a sharp knife score the orange with 8 equally spaced vertical cuts. Slip your thumb under the peel at the top and pull off the peel in 8 sections; set aside. The pulp will not be used in this recipe, so you can eat it while you prepare the cake. Preheat the oven to 350°.

Generously butter a 9 x 9 x 2-inch pan (or 10-inch DO). If you are using the wine icing, line the bottom of the pan with wax paper and butter the paper; set aside 1 section of the orange peel for the icing, reserving the remaining 7 for the cake. (If you are using the orange glaze, do not line the pan with wax paper and use all 8 of the orange peel sections in the cake.)

Mix in a food processor if you have one, the flour, raisins, baking soda and salt. Process the orange peel sections with 1/2 c. sugar until the peel is fine, or do this by hand if you do not have a food processor. Add to flour mixture. Mix remaining sugar and butter until smooth and light in color. Add the eggs, one at a time. Add the buttermilk and vanilla. Add the finely chopped walnuts. Add the flour mixture and mix all the ingredients until the flour just disappears. Put batter in pan and bake in a preheated oven for 30 to 35 minutes or until a toothpick in the center comes out clean.

If you are using the orange glaze, prepare while the cake is baking and spoon it evenly over the cake. Return the cake to the oven for 5 minutes. Cool in the pan on a wire rack. If you are using the wine icing cool the cake in the pan on a wire rack for 10 minutes. Turn out onto the rack and let cool completely before icing. Spread the icing evenly over the top and sides.

Orange Glaze

Makes about 1/2 cup.

1/2 cup sugar   3 T orange juice

In a small bowl stir together the sugar and orange juice.

Wine Icing

Makes 1 1/4 cup.

2 cups confectioners' sugar   1 large egg white
reserved section of orange peel from orange wine cake recipe   3 to 4 t dry sherry
5 T unsalted butter, at room temperature

Mince orange peel and mix with the sugar. Add the butter and mix. Add the egg white and mix. Add the sherry. If the icing is too thick to be spread easily, add up to 1 t more sherry, little by little, until proper consistency.

Before Trip:

- Prepare beef kabobs and freeze in ZLB.
- Buy sweet pickles 1 day before trip and transfer to either a ZLB with a small amount of the pickle juice, or in a plastic container depending on available space.
- Buy spinach 1 day before trip. Wash and dry, put in a ZLB with a few paper towels.
- Buy red onion and store in ZLB or cool dark place.
- Buy walnuts and put in ZLB.
- Buy poppy seed dressing and transfer to a plastic bottle.
- Buy flat noodles and put whole package in ZLB.
- Make Orange Wine Cake 1 week before your trip. Cool cake, wrap in plastic a few times and freeze.
- For Orange Glaze, put sugar in ZLB. Store the orange in a cool place for your 3 T of orange juice.
- For Wine Icing, make this 1 day before your trip and put in a plastic container. Take a little extra sherry along and add to icing if it becomes too thick to spread on cake, or for sipping/medicinal purposes. You get the idea.

On Trip: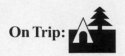

- Make Brie Pinwheel.
- Make sure your beef tips and cake are not frozen the day before you make your kabobs.
- Start fire for grilling kabobs.
- Get out cake and wrap loosely in foil.
- Put together kabobs and put on grill. Don't forget to use the marinade to baste the kabobs.
- Make salad and set it out with the poppy seed dressing.
- Open wine and set out ready to serve.
- Put cake in foil on or near grill so that it can gets lightly warm, about room temperature.
- Make sure frosting is right consistency by adding sherry if necessary. Frost cake.
- Make noodles according to instructions.
- Serve food buffet style and let everyone pick out their own kabob. That way you're sure to have satisfied customers.
- Cut and serve the cake. What a delicious meal.

Menu Eleven

Days 1 - 4

Breakfast

Scrambled Eggs with Sausage and Thyme

Seasonal Fruits

Dried Tart Cherry and Almond Muffins

Lunch

Summer Couscous Salad

Oriental Crackers

Red and Green Grapes

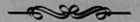

Dinner

Dates with Crème Fraiche and Roasted Walnuts

Pan Fried Trout or Foil-Wrapped Trout with Lemon

Toasted Walnut Vinaigrette Salad

Hot Biscuits

Hatch Chile Apple Cobbler

Alsatian Riesling or Chenin Blanc

Scrambled eggs
with Sausage and Thyme

Serves 4.
Cream cheese gives this a nice texture.

8 large eggs
1 T coarse-grained mustard (I use Dijon)
1/8 t salt
1/2 t ground black pepper
3 T butter
4 oz. fully cooked smoked turkey sausage,
or your favorite cooked sausage, quartered lengthwise, thinly sliced crosswise

1/2 cup chopped green onions or red onion
2 t dried thyme
4-oz. Neufchatel cheese (reduced fat cream cheese), cut into small cubes
fresh thyme sprigs for garnish (opt.)

Whisk eggs, mustard, salt and pepper. Melt 1 T of butter in a 12-inch diameter nonstick skillet over medium heat. Add sausage and stir until brown about 3 minutes. Add onion and thyme and stir 1 minute. Transfer mixture to a bowl or plate. Melt 2 T of butter in same skillet over medium heat. Add eggs and stir 1 or 2 minutes; then add cheese and sausage; stir until eggs are how you like them. Personally, I like them hard and rubbery so if you sling them at a wall they would bounce off. When I order them at a restaurant you can see why the people who take our order give me strange looks.

Dried Tart Cherry and Almond Muffins

Serves 10.
I really like the almond flavor with the dried cherries but you could use other dried fruits, experiment. The almond paste also adds moisture.

6 T orange juice
3/4 cup dried tart cherries (about 4-oz.)
6 T (3/4 stick) unsalted butter, melted, hot
1 7-oz. package almond paste
3 large eggs, can be powdered
1 1/2 t grated orange peel, fresh if possible

1 cup plus 2 T flour
1/4 cup sugar
1/2 t baking powder
1/4 t salt
1 10-inch DO or muffin pans (10 cup)

Butter your DO. If making at home, preheat oven to 375°. Bring orange juice to a simmer in small pan. Add cherries; let stand about 10 minutes. Mix hot butter and almond paste until well blended. Add eggs one at a time, beating well after each addition. Mix in cherries and orange peel. Add flour, sugar, baking powder and salt. Mix just until blended. Pour batter into greased DO or muffin pans. Bake until tester inserted into center comes out clean, about 20-25 minutes. This can be prepared two days ahead. Cool. Wrap in foil and store at room or outdoor temperature. Reheat in foil in a DO, over steaming water, or a grill at 350° for 5-10 minutes.

If using powdered eggs just add this to the flour mixture in your ZLB, but remember to add the proper amount of liquid to the batter when the recipe calls for the eggs.

Before trip:

- Don't forget the eggs.
- Don't forget to get seasonal fruits to slice up.
- Measure and put all dry ingredients into a ZLB.
- Put butter in ZLB.
- You can use the orange juice you mix up for breakfast.

On Trip:

- Slice fruit.
- Make muffins.
- Make eggs.

Summer Couscous Salad

Serves 7.

This is a different version of the classic Moroccan dish. It adds a little culture to your trip. You can serve this hot or cold. I prefer it cold.

4 cups chicken broth	12-oz. of zucchini, trimmed and chopped (about 2 cups)
1/4 cup plus 2 T olive oil	9-oz. of carrots, trimmed, peeled and chopped (about 1 cup)
1/4 t turmeric	3-oz. of onions peeled and chopped (about 1/2 cup)
1/4 t cinnamon	1 large tomato (about 12-oz.) chopped, seeded (opt.)
1/4 t powdered ginger	15-oz. canned garbanzo beans, drained
2 cups couscous (dry precooked semolina cereal)	1 1/2 T fresh lemon juice
	1/2 t salt
1/2 cup dark raisins	1/2 cup toasted slivered almonds
1/2 cup chopped dates	

In a 4-quart pan, bring the broth, 1/4 cup of oil, turmeric, cinnamon, and ginger to a boil. Gradually stir in couscous; boil another 1 to 2 minutes until the liquid is absorbed. Remove from heat; stir in raisins and dates. Cover tightly and let stand for 15 minutes. Transfer couscous to a large mixing bowl to cool until room temperature. Add zucchini, carrots, onion, tomato and garbanzo beans. In a small bowl, combine 2 T oil, lemon juice and salt. Pour over salad and toss well. Cover and refrigerate overnight to blend flavors. Before serving, sprinkle with almonds. Kept in a cooler, this will last in a ZLB up to 8-9 days.

Before Trip:

- Make couscous, but leave out toasted almonds.
- Put toasted almonds in separate ZLB to be added on trip.
- Crackers should be in ZLB.
- Wash grapes, dry completely, and keep dry or they could mold. Put in ZLB with paper towels the day before you leave on your trip.

On Trip:

- Set out couscous and add toasted almonds.
- Set out crackers.
- Set out grapes.

Summer Couscous Salad, Page 94

Scouting Lava Falls (John Evans)

Dates with Crème Fraiche and Roasted Walnuts

Serves 6.
Of course you can use any dates, but Medjool dates are my favorite. The flavor of this combination tastes like pumpkin pie.

12 dates, seedless or with seeds
1/4 cup roasted walnuts (finely chopped)

4-oz. of Crème Fraiche (see Menu 10, Days 1-4, or buy at market)

Split dates and remove seeds, fill with Crème Fraiche, and sprinkle roasted walnuts on top.

Pan Fried Trout with Lemon

Serves 8.
The only way to eat wild trout is to go out and catch them yourself; otherwise you'll most likely be chowing down on farm-raised. Invite some avid fishing people on your trip. Mmmm good!

8 medium trout (about 9 to 10-oz. each), gutted and cleaned
3 1/2 t salt
1/2 t ground black pepper
1/2 cup flour

4 lemons, cut into 1/4-inch rounds
4 1/2 t butter
4 1/2 t olive oil
4 1/2 t sesame oil

Rinse trout and pat dry. Combine 2 t salt, 1/4 t pepper, and flour on a plate. Season insides of fish with remaining 1 1/2 t salt and 1/4 t pepper. Insert three slices of lemon inside each fish, and dredge in flour; shake off excess. Heat 1 1/2 t butter, 1 1/2 t olive oil, and 1 1/2 t sesame oil in an 11-inch skillet over medium high heat. Add three trout, arrange 4 or 5 lemon slices around fish and cook until golden brown, about 5 to 6 minutes. If lemon begins to burn, put them on top of fish. Turn fish, and cook until it has a golden crust and is flaky and moist, about 5 or 6 minutes. Remove fish from skillet and keep warm wrapped in foil. Repeat twice with remaining trout or use several skillets at once. Serve fish with cooked lemon slices.

Foiled Wrapped Trout with Lemon

I actually like this one because it is so easy. This is the way I ate my trout when fishing and camping in the mountains of Colorado. Simple, yet delicious. Those were the days when you could fish small lakes and the fish weren't used to seeing people. I would use a safety pin at the end of my boot lace with cheese to catch trout. What a great way to fish for trout.

8 medium trout
1 stick of butter
4 large lemons

salt and pepper to taste
3 chopped tomatoes (opt.)
foil

Clean trout as in previous recipe. Lightly butter four pieces of foil (two trout per piece of foil). Lay trout in foil. Salt and pepper inside and outside of trout. Squeeze 1/2 lemon inside and outside of trout. Put little pieces of butter over and inside of each trout. Sprinkle chopped tomatoes over trout. Seal foil and put on coals 1-2 minutes per side or on grill 4-5 minutes on each side. Test with a fork to see if fish is flaky. Unwrap and eat the most delicate and tasty trout of your life.

Toasted Walnut Vinaigrette Salad

Makes 3/4 cup.

2 T Dijon mustard
3 T red wine vinegar
7 T walnut oil
salt and freshly ground pepper, to taste
1/2 to 3/4 cup walnuts, toasted
lettuce or salad greens

Whisk together the mustard and vinegar. Gradually add oil in a slow, steady stream as you continue to whisk ingredients. Season with salt and pepper. Toss this dressing with any type of lettuce greens and add toasted walnuts. Simple and delicious.

Hatch Chile Apple Cobbler

When you think of peppers you don't normally think of desserts, especially a cobbler. I assure you this recipe is delicious and will certainly get your creative juices flowing.

Filling:

5-6 Granny Smith apples peeled, sliced
2/3 cup packed brown sugar
1/4-1/2 cup chopped roasted and peeled Hatch
or other mild chile peppers, I prefer fresh chiles
1 t cider vinegar

1/4 t cinnamon
1/4 t salt
1/8 t allspice
1/8 t nutmeg

Cobbler Topping:

1 cup sugar
1 1/4 cup flour
1/8 t salt
1/8 t cinnamon

1/8 t nutmeg
grated zest of 2 lemons (opt.)
3/4 cup butter
2 T milk or heavy cream

For the filling:

Combine the apples, brown sugar, chiles, vinegar, cinnamon, salt, allspice, nutmeg in a bowl and mix well. Spoon into a greased 10-inch DO.

For the topping:

Combine the sugar, flour, salt, cinnamon and nutmeg, and lemon zest in a bowl and mix well. Cut in the butter until the mixture is crumbly. Stir in milk/cream. Spread over the apple filling and press firmly. Bake at 375° for about 35-40 minutes or until brown and bubbly.

Before Trip:

- Put dates in ZLB.
- Put container of Crème Fraiche in ZLB. Keep refrigerated.
- Roast walnuts in toaster oven or on cookie sheet in oven just until brown. Cool and finely chop. Put in ZLB the day before trip. Keep refrigerated.
- Buy fresh trout and freeze in ZLB or catch your own. It is worth the effort to fish in a river and lots of fun. If you freeze trout before your trip, do so in a block of ice, it will last longer. We have frozen in milk cartons or a large ZLB.
- Put dry ingredients in ZLB.
- Put whole lemons in ZLB.
- Put butter in ZLB for fish, biscuits, and cobbler.
- Put olive oil in small plastic bottle.
- Put sesame oil in small plastic bottle.
- Don't forget the foil for the fish.
- Make Walnut Oil Vinaigrette. Put in plastic bottle.
- Day before trip, wash lettuce and dry. Put in ZLB with paper towels.
- Buy biscuits in a can and put can in ZLB in refrigerator. Allow two biscuits per person.
- Buy apples, wash.
- For cobbler filling combine all dry ingredients in a ZLB.
- Put chiles in ZLB.
- Cider vinegar in plastic container in ZLB.
- Combine dry ingredients in ZLB for cobbler topping.
- Put milk or cream in plastic container in ZLB. If using powdered milk put in with dry ingredients and add a little water when making.

On Trip:

- Chill wine in river or cooler.
- Make dates and set out.
- Start coals for DO.
- Make sure the fish is thawed if using frozen. Check a day or two in advance.
- Make cobbler in DO and start baking.
- Put biscuits in DO.
- Bake fish and keep warm in foil, when this is almost done, start biscuits baking.
- Make salad and set out.
- Be sure you keep your eyes and nose on the DO.

97

Menu One
Days 5 - 12

Breakfast

Quickie Quiche

Apple Currant Bread

Lunch

Marinated Crab Salad in Lettuce Wraps

Assorted Crackers

Fig Newton Cookies

Dinner

Bulgur Dip with Pita Bread Chips

Grilled Ginger Chicken

Salad with Toasted Pecans, Cranberries, and Stilton

Angel Rolls

Chocolate Cinnamon Cake

Gewurztraminer Wine

For the Days 5-12 menus you will still be able to use some perishables, but not as many meat dishes or fresh salads.

Quickie Quiche

Serves 5.

2 cups Bisquick
1 cup milk, can use powdered milk
3 eggs, can use powered or egg substitutes
Adoba, or any other type of seasoning, be creative
1/2 to 3/4 lb of sausage (opt.)
3/4 cup Parmesan cheese

This is a very simple but good recipe. Brown sausage in a small DO, sprinkle Parmesan cheese over sausage, set aside. If you decide not to use sausage make sure the bottom of your DO is lightly greased with oil. Mix first 4 ingredients in a bowl, then add to the sausage mixture, and place hot coals on top and underneath the DO. Cook until you smell something wonderful, about 20-30 min. Remember you can always lift the lid and check to see when done. Hint: always rely on your nose when making anything in a DO.

Apple Currant Bread

Makes 2 medium loaves, about 1 pound each.
I like this bread because it isn't too sweet and it freezes well so that you can make it in advance.

2 cups white flour
1 t baking soda
1 T baking powder
1 t salt
1 t cinnamon
1/4 t freshly grated nutmeg
2/3 cup dried currants
1/2 cup (1 stick) unsalted butter, room temperature, cut into 4 pieces

1 cup sugar
3 large eggs
1 T fresh lemon juice
1 t vanilla extract
2 t lemon zest
2 Granny Smith apples (or other tart apples), peeled, cored, and diced

Grease and lightly flour two 4-cup bread pans. Preheat oven to 350. Adjust oven rack to center position. In a bowl, mix first 7 ingredients. Set aside. In a mixing bowl cream together butter and sugar, add the eggs and continue to mix. Add lemon juice, vanilla, and zest. Mix until fluffy. Stir in dry ingredients and apples. Mix until flour disappears. Do not over mix. Spoon batter into pans and spread evenly. Bake for 40-45 minutes until browned. Cool in pan 10 minutes. Turn out onto wire rack and allow to cool completely before freezing.

Before Trip:

- Measure out Bisquick and put in ZLB with recipe, or you can buy Bisquick in small packages.
- You can put powdered milk in same ZLB with Bisquick, or use real milk and put in a plastic bottle and keep cold, or sterile milk (see Tips).
- If you use powdered eggs also add to the above ZLB. If fresh eggs, crack into a plastic bottle and keep cold. Do this the day before your trip begins.
- Make apple currant bread and freeze.

On Trip:

- Make quiche.
- When quiche is finished, slice in DO, set out apple currant bread and let people dig in. Bread is best when it is warm.

Marinated Crab Salad in Lettuce Wraps

Serves 4.

1 lb lump crabmeat (canned)	2 T chopped fresh basil
1 carrot, finely diced	juice of two limes
1 T capers	3 T olive oil
3 green onions, white and green, finely chopped	Tabasco sauce
2 T chopped fresh parsley	1 head iceberg lettuce

Mix all ingredients being careful not to break up the crab meat too much. Put a tablespoon or more on a lettuce leaf and roll up. Everyone can make their own lettuce wrap. A light, easy, scrumptious meal.

Before Trip:

- Nothing to prepare in advance other than shopping for ingredients.

On Trip:

- Prepare wraps.
- Make sure people have spoons and cups or plates to eat on.
- Set out the crackers and Fig Newtons and enjoy an easy but delicious lunch.

Bulgur Dip with Pita Bread Chips

Makes 7 cups, 1/4 cup per person is usually enough for appetizers.

This dip is one of my personal favorites because it is easy, tasty, freezes well, and, it satisfies meat lovers and vegetarians. Make it and you will see why.

2 cups fine bulgur	2 cups olive oil
1 cup loosely packed parsley leaves	1/4 cup tamarind syrup (oriental store)
2 onions peeled and finely diced	2 t ground cumin
1 8-oz. can tomato sauce	1/2 t cayenne
6 T tomato paste (3oz.)	salt and freshly ground black pepper
2 cups pine nuts (lightly roasted)	pita bread chips or crackers

Soak the bulgur in a large bowl with water to cover until most of the water is absorbed and the bulgur is soft, about 2 hours. Finely chop the parsley leaves and the onion. Put in a large bowl and reserve. Squeeze out the excess water from the bulgur in a towel and add the bulgur to the parsley and onion, along with the rest of the ingredients in the bowl. Adjust seasoning. Serve with the pita chips, crackers, or anything else your heart desires.

Grilled Ginger Chicken

Serves 4.

1 chicken (about 3 lbs), cut into 4 pieces	1/2 to 3/4 t freshly ground black pepper
1 piece peeled fresh ginger, about 1 x 1 x 2 inch	2 t dried thyme
1 garlic clove	1/4 t salt
1/4 cup fresh lemon juice	1 bay leaf, broken into small pieces
2 T oil	

Put the chicken pieces in one layer in a low, flat dish, skin side up. Finely chop the ginger and garlic by hand or in a food processor. Add the remaining ingredients and mix or process. Pour over the chicken and let stand 2 hours in the refrigerator. Put all in ZLB and freeze. Will keep for 1-2 months.

Salad With Pecans, Cranberries, and Stilton

Serves 6.
This is one of my all time favorite salads. I think you will see what I mean if you decide to make it.

1 small head iceberg lettuce (keeps longer than others)
6 oz. Stilton cheese

1 cup dried cranberries
salt and pepper to taste

Pecans

1/2 T orange rind, grated
1/8 cup orange juice

1/4 cup sugar
2 cups toasted pecan halves

In a saucepan, bring the first three ingredients to a boil. Add the pecans. Stir constantly with a slotted spoon for 3-5 minutes, being careful not to burn the pecans. Place pecans on waxed paper to cool. Use one cup in the salad and freeze or snack on the rest.

Sherry Vinaigrette Dressing

3 t Grey Poupon Dijon mustard
3/4 t sugar
3 T Spanish sherry wine vinegar

6 T olive oil
salt and pepper

Make sure lettuce is clean and patted dry. Whisk together mustard, sugar, and vinegar. Slowly drizzle olive oil into mixture whisking constantly. Add salt and pepper to taste. Toss dressing with lettuce and top with cranberries, crumbled Stilton, and pecans.

Angel Rolls

Makes 5 dozen.

5 2/3 cups of flour	1 cup shortening, Crisco
1/3 cup whole wheat flour	1 package dry yeast
1/4 cup sugar	1/4 cup warm water
1 T baking powder	2 cups buttermilk
1 t baking soda	2 cups butter, melted (opt.)
1 t salt	

Sift dry ingredients; cut in shortening with a knife or pastry cutter; dissolve yeast in warm water and add with buttermilk to dry ingredients. Mix well. Knead on a floured surface until smooth and satiny; roll out 1/4 inch thick on a floured board. Cut with round cutter (2 to 3 inch), dip in melted butter (opt.), fold in half, and place on cookie sheet. At this point you may: bake at 400° for 12 - 15 minutes, put in refrigerator to bake later in day, or put in freezer and when frozen put in a ZLB. You can also take the leftover dough and roll it thin, spread with melted butter, sugar, and cinnamon, roll it up, slice it, and bake as cinnamon rolls. These can also be frozen. I love these little rolls because not only do they do well on raft trips, but you can pull them out of the freezer anytime and have fresh homemade rolls. A real winner with last minute guests.

Chocolate Cinnamon Cake

Serves 10-12.
Easy, moist, and delicious.

2 cups flour	2 cups buttermilk
2 cups sugar	2 eggs, beaten
1 stick butter	1 T soda
4 T powdered cocoa	1 T cinnamon
1 cup water	1 t vanilla

Mix flour and sugar in a bowl. Boil butter, cocoa, and water in a pan. Pour this into the flour mixture. Add the rest of the ingredients and stir until smooth. Pour all into a lightly greased and floured 12-inch DO. Bake 350° for 35 minutes.

Icing

1 stick butter
4 T powdered cocoa
6 T milk
1 box powdered sugar
1 cup chopped nuts (opt.)
1 T vanilla

Bring to a boil butter, cocoa, and milk. Remove from heat and add powdered sugar, nuts, and vanilla. Spread on cake in pan when cooled. This can be made ahead and put into a plastic container in your cooler. Yummy!

Before Trip:

- Make the bulgur dip. Put in a ZLB and freeze. This will last 2-3 months in the freezer.
- Marinate chicken and freeze.
- Make pecans and sherry vinaigrette.
- Make angel rolls and freeze.
- To make the cake, put flour and sugar in a ZLB. Put powered cocoa in ZLB. Put buttermilk (if powdered), eggs (if powdered), soda, cinnamon, and vanilla(must be well mixed) in a ZLB. You can use real buttermilk or eggs, just put them in their own separate plastic containers. Make sure they are kept in a cooler. The icing can be made a week in advance of your trip and stored in the refrigerator in a ZLB or plastic container. Or it can be made on the river. I always prefer to do as much as possible before hand so I have more free time to enjoy friends, river, and the fabulous scenery.

On Trip:

- Make sure your bulgur dip is thawed a day before you serve it. You can even take it out of your cooler the morning of the day you plan on serving it. Put the dip and chips/crackers in a nice dish and set out prior to dinner for those hungry appetites.
- Prepare your charcoal for the grill and 2 DOs (10-inch and 12-inch). The grill for the chicken and the DOs for the rolls and cake.
- Take defrosted chicken out of cooler and set aside.
- Lightly grease both DOs.
- Take defrosted rolls from ZLB and place in small, lightly greased DO.
- Mix up cake batter and put in large DO .
- Make the salad.
- When coals are ready put the large DO on the bottom with coals on top and bottom, then set small DO on top with coals on the lid. Remember to save coals for grilling your chicken.
- Put chicken on the grill and turn as needed. Chicken usually takes 20-30 minutes on a charcoal grill depending on the size.
- Set out your icing ready to spread.
- Set up your table with room for a plate of chicken, salad bowl, and rolls served in a DO.
- When you start smelling the rolls immediately take the small DO off the fire and set aside. The same goes for the cake. Remember you can always lift the lid to check to see that foods do not burn. Set all food out at once and start opening and serving the wine.
- When you are finished eating, the cake should be cool enough to add the frosting. Bring it to the table and serve. People will praise you for a great meal.

Menu Two

Days 5 - 12

Breakfast

Cottage Scrambled Eggs

Oatmeal-Banana/Apple Muffins

Lunch

Pesto Macaroni Salad

Tangerines and Chocolate Bars

Dinner

Cheese Board with Crackers and Nuts

Marinated Chicken Supreme

Maple Baked Onions

Salad of Greens

Upside Down Apple Tart

Riesling or Sauvignon Blanc

Cottage Scrambled Eggs

Serves 4.
Simple, good, and easy.

3 T butter	10 eggs
1 small onion, chopped	1 cup cottage cheese
3 T flour	salt and pepper to taste
1 cup milk	

Melt butter in a skillet and sauté the onion. Add flour and stir. Add milk slowly and whisk until you have a smooth cream sauce. Combine eggs, cottage cheese, salt, and pepper. Stir into sauce. Cook stirring occasionally until eggs are firm. (Too much stirring gives eggs a grainy texture.)

Oatmeal-Banana/Apple Muffins

Serves 8-10.

1 cup plus 2 T quick cooking rolled oats	1/2 t nutmeg (freshly grated nutmeg is best)
1 cup buttermilk (powdered or liquid)	1/4 cup walnuts, coarsely chopped
1 t vanilla	1 large banana, coarsely chopped,
1 cup unbleached flour	or 1 medium tart apple, unpeeled, cored, chopped
2 t baking soda	1 large egg
1 T baking powder	2 cups brown sugar
1 t salt	1/4 cup (1/2 stick) butter
1/4 t cinnamon	

If you want to make these ahead of time, freeze, and put in a ZLB, make sure you will have room in your cooler because they do require a lot of space. I prefer to make them on the river because there is nothing like waking up to fresh baked goods in the wilderness.

For making ahead of time:
Grease 18 muffin cups, 1/3-cup capacity. Preheat oven to 400°. Adjust rack to middle of oven. Mix oats, buttermilk, and vanilla in a bowl. Set aside. In another bowl, mix the egg and brown sugar, then add the melted butter. Stir in oat mixture, and then add the flour, baking soda, baking powder, salt, cinnamon, nutmeg, chopped walnuts, and banana. Stir just until the flour disappears. Be careful not to over stir. Spoon into muffin cups, filling 2/3 full. Sprinkle top of batter with additional cinnamon. Bake in oven for 18 minutes. Remove muffins from pans and cool on wire rack.

For making on the river:
Combine all dry ingredients, including powdered buttermilk and egg into a ZLB and put recipe inside. Mix vanilla into brown sugar thoroughly, put in ZLB and put inside bag with dry ingredients. Put your 2 sticks of butter in a ZLB and label. Or use squeeze margarine on the river. Make sure you take a very green banana if you will not be using it for several days or take an apple, or even raisins, dried cranberries or cherries if you feel a little lazy. This can all be made in a greased 12-inch DO very easily. But since it will be like one large muffin, bake at 350° instead of 400°. Remember, the key is when you start to smell the muffins check to see if it is done. So get someone who has a good sniffer and put him/her to work.

Pesto Macaroni Salad

Serves 6.
This is really easy. Just buy the pesto, 1 cup per 16-oz bag of macaroni or other pasta. Or if you want to make your own, here's how.

Pesto *(makes 2 cups).*

2 cups fresh basil leaves firmly packed (about 4 bunches)	1/2 t salt
1 Tb minced garlic (about 3 cloves)	1/2 t pepper
1/2 cup pine nuts or toasted walnuts or pecans	1/2 cup olive oil
1/2 cup fresh grated Parmesan cheese	2 16-oz. packages macaroni

Puree all ingredients except macaroni in a blender or food processor. Transfer to a container or ZLB and label. This will stay fresh in the frig for up to 2 months, and frozen up to a year. You can also use this to flavor soups, grilled meats, or chicken. It is also good on steamed vegetables or new potatoes. I'm sure you can think of many other uses for pesto as well.

Cook pasta according to directions on package, add pesto, and refrigerate.

Before Trip:

- Buy or make pesto & freeze.

On Trip:

- Cook pasta and add pesto. Put in cooler the morning of the day you are going to serve it.
- Remind people to have a plate and utensil handy at lunch time.
- Set out chocolate bars and tangerines and watch everything disappear quickly.

Marinated Chicken Supreme

Serves 6.

Marinade for 6 large chicken breasts or 1 whole chicken (if grilling I use chicken with the skin on as it keeps the chicken more moist, you can always remove the skin after cooking).

2 cups pineapple juice	1/2 T black pepper
2 t ginger	2 t Dijon mustard or your favorite
1 t garlic salt or fresh minced garlic	2 cups soy sauce (lite is fine)
1 T brown sugar	1/4 cup canola oil

Simmer all for 5 minutes, cool. Put chicken in MSB and add marinade, and freeze. Put at the bottom of your cooler next to ice or dry ice. It will thaw out in several days but will last in the cooler, thawed out, 4 to 5 days. Be sure and keep it as cold as possible. If having it later, consider adding 1/4 cup vodka to the marinade as preservative.

Maple Baked Onions

Serves 6.
Easy, easy, easy, and tasty.

3 medium sweet onions, Texas 1015s, Walla Wallas, or any other great tasting onion
1/2 - 3/4 cup maple syrup, and not the fake stuff

Put 1/8-inch water in a 12-inch DO. Peel onions, cut in half, and place in DO with cut side facing up. Put lid on and add 6 coals underneath and 16 on top. Cook about 20 minutes, take lid off and if onions pieces are starting to separate drizzle maple syrup on top of onions. Replace lid and cook 20 more minutes and check to see if they are somewhat soft. If so, they are finished unless you like them a little more crisp. The timing will vary, so keep checking, it is worth the effort of removing the lid a few times. These can also be made at home in a toaster or regular oven. At home I usually let them bake for an hour.

Salad of Greens

Use any mixture of greens. There are many varieties to choose from these days. Iceberg keeps the longest, but if possible I use Boston, bibb, or oak leaf lettuce with Belgian endive or watercress. Or how about romaine with radicchio or fresh spinach? You can even buy bagged, pre-washed mixed greens and not have to do anything but bring the bag along. Otherwise, the day before your trip, wash the greens, dry, and put in a ZLB with paper towels. Store in the frig.

You could either buy your favorite dressing or make the following simple vinaigrette:

1 T red or white wine vinegar, or balsamic vinegar	pinch of oregano or basil
1/4 t salt, or to taste	1 t Dijon mustard
1/4 t fresh ground pepper, or to taste	3 T virgin or extra virgin olive oil

Combine all ingredients in a jar and shake well. It will last several weeks in the frig, so you can make it well in advance.

Upside-Down Apple Tart

Serves 8.

This dessert is so easy and delicious that you will want to make it at home and probably all the time. The French name for this delight is Tarte Tatin. It was invented in a restaurant on the Loire River in France by the Tatin sisters. I've adapted it so that it can be prepared easily on the river.

Pie dough:

Buy dough in flat, 8-9 inch rounds pre-made at the grocery store, usually in the frozen section. Or sometimes it comes in sticks like butter. I prefer to make my own pie dough ahead of time, roll it out in an 8-inch circle and freeze it until it is time for the trip.

1 cup white flour	1/3 cup Crisco
1/4 tsp. salt	4-5 T ice water

Put flour and salt in a bowl. Cut in Crisco with a knife or pastry blender until it resembles small peas or coarse grain, then add water, 1 T at a time. Gently toss with a fork. Repeat until all is moistened and you can form a ball. Flatten on a lightly floured surface until you have a 4-inch circle, and then with a rolling pin make an 8-inch circle. Fold dough in half, then quarters, lift and put on a piece of plastic wrap on a cookie sheet, and put in freezer for 20-30 minutes. Remove from freezer and wrap entire circle in plastic and put in a large ZLB and freeze.

Apple Filling:

6-7 golden delicious apples,
peeled and sliced lengthwise, not too thin
grated rind of 1 lemon
1 T lemon juice

1/4 cup sugar
6 T (3/4 stick) butter, cut in pieces
1 cup sugar

Mix first four ingredients in a bowl. Wait about 15 minutes until all juice has been rendered, then drain. Heat 10-inch DO over low-med heat with butter and 1 cup sugar. Stir several minutes with a wooden spoon, until mixture turns a good caramel brown. Remove from heat and arrange a layer of apple slices nicely on the bottom of the pan to make an attractive design. Put the rest of the apples on top, close-packed but not neat. They sink down as they cook. Set the DO back on the stove over moderate-high heat, pressing apples down as they soften, and drawing juices up over them as they continue to cook. Cover the DO and continue cooking 10-15 minutes, until juices are thickened and syrupy. Remove from heat. Place dough on top, cut four steam holes, ¼-inch across near the center. Bake 20-25 minutes at about 350° until the wonderful aroma starts driving you mad. Now you're ready to serve it up. You can turn it upside down on a serving plate; this always impresses everyone, or you can slice it right from the DO and turn each piece upside down. Top with sour cream, whipped cream, crème fraiche, or even vanilla ice cream if you can keep it on dry ice.

It isn't impossible to do this with some advance planning. After this, people will think you should go into the restaurant business.

Before Trip:

- Prepare marinated chicken.
- Store onions in a mesh bag.
- Put maple syrup in plastic container.
- Buy greens day before the trip and prepare as needed.
- Make or buy dressing and put in plastic container.
- Make or buy pie dough. Don't forget to take a rolling pin, or you can use a drinking cup or glass for rolling out your dough.
- I try to put apples in a ZLB in the cooler. If space is a problem, you may have to store them in your dry box, but as cooler space becomes available, you should move them.
- Mix grated lemon rind, sugar, and lemon juice, put in ZLB and label the day before the trip.

On Trip:

- Make sure the chicken is thawed the day before grilling.
- Slice or set out cheeses with crackers on a cutting board. If time permits, I make some sort of arrangement of flowers, driftwood, leaves, whatever you can find in nature, to decorate the cheese board. Put out nuts in a bowl, or in anything that brings on a festive mood. Use your imagination!
- Start your charcoal immediately for your chicken and maple onions.
- Prepare DO and onions for cooking.
- When coals are ready, bake onions in large DO. After onions have been baking about 20 minutes, start grilling chicken.
- Prepare salad.
- Prepare dessert.
- People can serve themselves; just make sure you have the tongs out for the chicken and maybe a large spoon for the baked onions and salad.
- While dessert is baking, everyone should be enjoying the dinner. Don't forget to uncork the wine!
- Serve dessert with your favorite topping or without; it is still just as mouth watering.

Menu Three

Days 5 - 12

Breakfast

Mexican Corn Bread Souffle

Bacon

Sliced Oranges with Currants and Coconut

Lunch

Apple Dip

Spinach Onion Caponata with Whole Wheat Tortillas

Betty's Oatmeal Cookies

Dinner

Pretzels with Honey Mustard

Mom's Meat Loaf

Hot Rolls

Fruitcake

Cabernet Sauvignon

Mexican Cornbread Soufflé

Serves 6-8.
Although this is easy, it requires some baking time.

1 cup creamed corn	1/2 t salt
2 eggs, beaten	1/2 t baking soda
1/3 cup corn oil	1 4-oz. can green chiles seeded & diced
3/4 cup milk	1 1/2 cups grated sharp cheddar cheese
1 cup cornmeal	

Start coals for DO. Lightly grease a 10-inch DO. Combine corn, eggs, oil, and milk. Mix cornmeal, salt, & soda together and add to milk mixture, blending well. Pour half the batter into the DO, spread chiles on mixture and sprinkle with half the cheese. Pour on remaining batter and remaining cheese. Bake 20-25 minutes or until you smell the fine aroma.

Before Trip:

- Combine all dry ingredients together in a ZLB.
- Eggs-refer to tips in front of book.
- Put block of cheese in ZLB.

On Trip:

- Fire up the coals.
- Mix the soufflé and bake.
- Slice fruit and mix with currants and coconut.
- Fry bacon.

Apple Dip

Makes 2 cups.

8-oz. cream cheese, slightly softened
1/2 cup brown sugar
1 1/2 t vanilla

1/2 cup roasted or honey roasted peanuts
red and green apples, sliced

Mix well and serve with apple slices.

Spinach Onion Caponata
with Whole Wheat Tortillas

Serves 5-6.

Caponata is a variation of ratatouille, an Italian vegetable dish. It travels well, freezes beautifully, and can be served cold or slightly warm. Will last in a cooler for three weeks. I make this up in advance, put in MSB and freeze it along with the tortillas wrapped separately. Toast and package pine nuts in a separate ZLB. Add to Caponata before using on tortillas.

1/2 cup olive oil
1/2 to 1 lb eggplant, peeled and cut into 1-inch cubes
1 large green bell pepper, cut into 1-inch pieces
1 large onion, diced
1 clove garlic, minced
1 15-oz. can diced tomatoes, undrained
3 T red wine vinegar
1 T sugar
1 T capers

1 T tomato paste
1 t salt
1/4 cup chopped fresh parsley
1/4 cup pimiento-stuffed green olives, rinsed and thickly sliced
1/4 t freshly ground pepper
1 t crumbled dried basil
1/4 cup toasted pine nuts
4-oz. fresh spinach, washed and dried
whole wheat tortillas

In a large, heavy saucepan combine first 6 ingredients and cook for about 20 to 30 minutes or until just tender. Add rest of ingredients except for the pine nuts, spinach, and tortillas. Cover and simmer for 15 minutes until most of juice has evaporated. Cool and put in ZLB in freezer. When ready to eat serve at room temperature with pine nuts and spinach.

Betty's Oatmeal Cookies

This is one of my husband's favorite cookies. His Mom is responsible for this recipe. They are moist and chewy, and the molasses gives it a great flavor. It's a winner!

Makes 5 dozen small cookies.

1/2 cup butter, softened	1 3/4 cup flour
1 1/4 cup sugar	1 t baking powder
1 t vanilla	1 t baking soda
6 T molasses	1/2 t salt
2 eggs	2 cups rolled oats, quick cooking

Mix butter, sugar, and vanilla, mix in molasses, then add eggs and stir. Sift flour, baking powder, soda and salt and add to mixture and stir until dry ingredients are wet. Then add rolled oats.

You can add any one of these: 1 cup raisins (my husband's favorite), 3/4 cup coconut, 3/4 cup chopped dates, 1/2 cup nuts, or 6-oz. chocolate chips. Drop by heaping tsp. about 4 inches apart on baking sheet and bake on center rack in oven at 325° for 12-15 minutes (until light brown). These freeze very well.

Before Trip:

- Make caponata.
- Make cookies and put in ZLB. Store in cooler if your trip is more than one week.
- Make apple dip and put in MSB. Add peanuts to dip just before serving.

On Trip:

- Set out apple dip and apple slices.
- Set out caponata, pine nuts, fresh spinach, and tortillas. Let everyone make a burrito.
- Set out yummy chewy oatmeal cookies.

Camp Chef! (John Evans)

Mom's Meatloaf, Page 117

Mom's Meat Loaf

Serves 4.

I grew up with this recipe. Mom had to be economical since there were nine children. It is simple but good. This was a lifesaver after flipping in Crystal rapid on the Grand Canyon many years ago.

1 lb ground beef	4 carrots
1/2 onion, diced	4 medium potatoes
2/3 cup oatmeal, quick cooking	2 medium onions
salt & pepper to taste	ketchup
1 egg	

Combine first 5 ingredients and blend well. Shape into an oval and put into a rectangular metal or glass pan with 1/4 cup water. Bake at 350° for 30 minutes. The meatloaf will be partially cooked. Let it cool, put in 2 large ZLBs, and freeze until trip.

On the trip, peel carrots and slice in half and then slice longwise. Peel potatoes and onions and cut into quarters. Put the meatloaf in a 12-inch DO and arrange the vegetables surrounding it. Add 1/2 to 3/4 cup water. Sprinkle salt and pepper over all. Add ketchup on top of meatloaf. Put lid on and bake about 40-50 minutes until vegetables are tender.

Before Trip:

- Make meatloaf and freeze.

On Trip:

- Make sure meatloaf is not frozen the day before you are to bake it.
- Start coals for meatloaf.
- Set out honey mustard in a nice dish and put pretzels around for dipping. Several varieties of pretzels are nice.
- Prepare vegetables with meatloaf and bake in DO.
- Break open refrigerator rolls (see Menu 4, Days 1-4), place in 10-inch greased DO, and bake over coals until done, approximately 15-20 minutes. Wait for the great aroma. Remember to start these baking only after the meatloaf has been baking at lest 20-25 minutes. You want everything ready to serve at the same time if possible.
- Serve everything from the DO. Mighty tasty.
- Slice and set out fruitcake. Get a good one, such as Corsicana (www.collinstreet.com) or Claxton (www.claxtonfruitcake.com); they are delicious, and pack a lot into a small package. Soak them with rum or brandy before your trip, if you like. Hot tea and/or port are a nice addition to this.

Menu Four
Days 5 - 12

Breakfast

Cold Cereals and Milk

Grits Souffle

Lunch

Spinach Dip Sandwiches with Pita & Oriental Slaw

Dried Apricots & Chocolate Bars

Dinner

Rosemary Walnuts

Elegant Boursin Pasta

Buttered Carrots

Baked Bread

Rustic Fruit Tart

Chardonnay, Pinot Blanc, or Pinot Noir

119

Grits Soufflé

Serves 6.

3/4 cup instant grits
3/4 cup milk
3/4 cup water
1/2 t salt

1/2 cup butter
6-oz. white sharp cheddar cheese, grated
3 eggs, lightly beaten

Place first four ingredients in a pan on stove. Cook, stirring occasionally, until moisture is absorbed. Place butter and grated cheese in 10-inch DO and add cooked grits, blending until cheese and butter are melted. Beat in eggs. Bake 20-25 minutes until slightly brown on top.

Before Trip:

- Put grits and salt in ZLB.
- If using powdered milk and/or eggs, those can be added to the same ZLB.

On Trip:

- Start coals.
- Mix soufflé and start baking.
- Set out cold cereals and milk.

Spinach Dip Sandwiches

Serves 6, (makes 3 cups).

10-oz. package frozen chopped spinach, thawed
1-1/2 cup plain yogurt, drained, or sour cream
1/2 cup mayonnaise
1 package (1.4-oz.) Knorr Tomato Pesto Soup Mix
1/4 cup fresh parsley, finely chopped (opt.)
pita bread

Squeeze spinach until dry. Stir all ingredients except bread together in bowl. Place in plastic container or ZLB if making ahead of time. Can be frozen. Will keep up to 1 week in cooler. Serve with pita bread.

Oriental Slaw

3 cups packaged shredded cabbage with carrots, or grate 1 small cabbage and 2 carrots	1 T sugar or maple syrup
	1 1/2 t toasted sesame oil
2 T salad oil	1 t soy sauce
4 t rice vinegar	1 t Dijon mustard

Place cabbage and carrot mixture in a bowl. Place all other ingredients in a sealable jar and shake well. Pour dressing over cabbage mixture.

This improves with age. Make the slaw and freeze in ZLB. Will keep up to 2 weeks in cooler.

Before Trip:

- Make spinach dip and freeze.
- Make oriental slaw and freeze.
- Freeze bread in ZLB.

On Trip:

- It is nice to put the dip and slaw into containers with spoons so that people can make their own sandwiches and serve themselves. Or if you are in a hurry, which I hope you aren't—after all, this is supposed to be a vacation—you can spoon it right out of the bag.
- Get out bread, dried fruit, and chocolate bars and eat up.

Rosemary Walnuts

This is great for happy hour.

3 T butter
1 t salt
2 cups walnuts

1/2 t ground rosemary
1/4 t cayenne pepper, or 1/2 t hot sauce

Preheat oven to 300°. Melt butter in a skillet and add remaining ingredients. Sauté walnuts for 5 minutes over medium heat stirring constantly so walnuts won't burn. Pour walnuts into a roasting pan or casserole dish and bake 20 min., stirring every 5 minutes. Cool and place in ZLB.

Elegant Boursin Pasta

Serves 6.
Quick and easy.

1 lb spinach or tomato fettuccine
3/4 cup milk

24-oz. Boursin cheese with garlic & herbs

Boil pasta according to package directions. In small saucepan, melt Boursin and milk over low heat. Drain pasta and pour melted cheese over pasta and toss. You can use just about any kind of soft cheese and spice combination, or other types of fettuccine.

Buttered Carrots

Serves 6.

10 carrots, peeled, sliced, and blanched*
salt & pepper to taste

4 1/2 T butter
2 T parsley flakes or fresh finely chopped parsley

Melt butter in pan, add carrots and sauté for 5 min, or until heated through. Add seasonings.
*To blanch, drop sliced carrots in boiling water for 1 min. Take out and run under cold water for 1 min. Put in ZLB. Can also freeze. Will keep 2 weeks in cooler.

Baked Bread

This is easy. Get the refrigerator bread that comes in the cans that you whack against the edge of the table to pop open. Take out your frustrations on that can. Place in lightly oiled DO and bake according to directions. Serve with the pasta.

Rustic Fruit Tart

Serves 8.

You can make this with cherries, plums, or rhubarb. Because of the mixture of nuts, sugar, and flour that lines the bottom of the tart, the fruit's juice will not turn the crust soggy.

1/2 cup walnuts (or other nuts)	3 16-oz. cans pitted bing cherries in heavy syrup
1/2 cup sugar	(or other soft fruit)
1/4 cup flour	2 T (1/4 stick) butter
pie dough for 1-crust pie	cherry brandy (opt.)

Before trip, in a blender or food processor, blend the walnuts and ¼ cup sugar. Add flour and blend to a fine powder. Put in ZLB and label. On trip, lightly flour surface, roll out pie dough to 12-inch circle, or 2-inch larger than diameter of DO. Place dough in DO and spread nut mixture evenly on top. Arrange cherries on top. Fold the rim of the dough up over the outermost fruit. Cut the butter into small pieces and distribute on top of the fruit. Sprinkle remaining ¼ cup sugar over fruit and the rim. Bake 40-45 minutes until crust is golden. After baking, sprinkle with cherry brandy.

Pie Dough

You can buy pre-made dough in sticks at the grocery store, or make it as follows.

2 cups flour	1/2 t salt
1 stick unsalted butter, cut into pieces	1 egg yolk
1 t sugar	1/3 cup cold water

Put flour, butter pieces, sugar, and salt in mixing bowl. With your fingers, loosely combine them to make a coarse meal, leaving the butter in distinct pieces. Add the yolk and water, mix by hand until the dough just comes together into a ball. Refrigerate until ready to use. You can make this in advance, place in labeled ZLB, and freeze.

Before Trip:

- Make rosemary walnuts. Put in ZLB and refrigerate or freeze.
- Make buttered carrots. Put in ZLB and freeze.
- Make pie dough. Put in ZLB and freeze.

On Trip:

- Set out rosemary walnuts.
- Start coals for bread and fruit tart.
- Make fruit tart and start baking.
- Start bread baking. Stack the tart and bread DOs and get double duty out of your coals. Put the bread DO on bottom and the tart on top, because the top DO gets more bottom heat, and the bread needs very little heat on the bottom.
- Make the pasta.
- When bread is ready, serve it with pasta, carrots, and wine.
- When fruit tart is done, remove coals and allow to cool a little before serving. I love this tart!

Menu Five
Days 5 - 12

Breakfast
Dad's Huevos Rancheros

Lunch
Wild Rice Tuna Salad

Pita, Chips, or Bread

Medjool Dates Stuffed with Mascarpone Cheese

Power Bars

Dinner
Curry Almond Spread with Crackers

Turkey-Tortilla Casserole

Green Salad with Toasted Pepitas and Pecans

Brown Sugar Orange Shortbread People

Riesling

Dad's Huevos Rancheros

This is my Dad's recipe. He tried to make this especially whenever anyone came down with a cold. In no time at all, it would clean out your sinuses with the many jalapenos he would add. I've toned it down a bit for those of you that aren't used to Texas heat.
Serves 8.

Sauce:

1/4 cup canola oil
2 large onions, chopped
3 large green bell peppers, chopped
3 cloves garlic, minced

2 jalapenos, minced
2 14.5-oz. cans diced tomatoes
2 8-oz. cans tomato sauce
salt and pepper to taste

Heat oil in large skillet, add onion and sauté, 8 minutes. Add bell peppers, garlic, and jalapenos and sauté another 5 minutes. Add canned tomatoes and tomato sauce and simmer for 1/2 hour. Add salt to taste. You can make this on the trip or put in MSB and freeze. It will keep in a cooler for three weeks if necessary.

Buy the Old El Paso (if available) Tostada Shells. They are already cooked and stay crisp in the package. Hopefully you can keep them in their packaging so they won't crumble. The other option is to fry corn tortillas in hot oil until crisp.

Refried beans come in cans. Or to make your own refer to Menu 3, Days 1-4. Guacamole can also be bought in packages or you can once again make your own.

3 T refried beans on each tortilla
1 to 2 fried eggs
rancheros sauce
3 T cheese per tortilla

2 T chopped tomato per tortilla (opt.)
1 T chopped onion per tortilla
3 T guacamole per tortilla
1 T sour cream (opt.)

To assemble: take a crisp tortilla and layer it with refried beans, a fried egg, rancheros sauce, grated Jack cheese, chopped tomatoes (opt.), chopped onions, and a dollop of guacamole and sour cream (opt.)on top. I load my tortillas up. Usually one per person is very filling. You can also put two eggs on your tortilla. Oh, momma is this ever good!

Before Trip:

- Make rancheros sauce.
- Purchase fresh produce.

On Trip:

- Heat sauce.
- Heat refried beans.
- Make guacamole or use pre-made .
- Grate cheese.
- Chop onions.
- Chop tomatoes (opt.).
- Fry eggs.

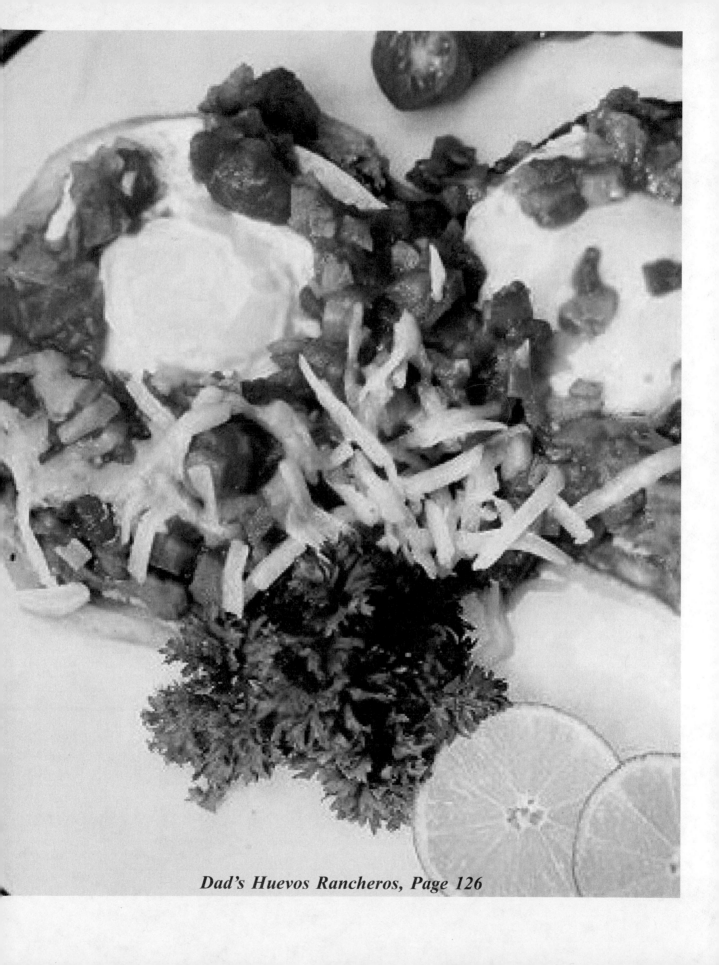

Dad's Huevos Rancheros, Page 126

Ledges Camp (James Machin)

Wild Rice Tuna Salad

Serves 8-10.

1 cup wild rice	1 cup chopped fresh parsley
4 ribs celery, chopped	2 to 4 T fresh lemon juice
2 large green bell peppers, chopped	black pepper to taste
2 large red bell peppers, chopped	3 12-oz. cans tuna
1 onion, finely chopped	bottle of creamy Italian dressing
3 cloves garlic, minced	

Combine 2 1/2 cups water with 1 cup wild rice. Simmer 35-40 minutes. Drain and cool. Chop ingredients. Mix all ingredients with rice and enough dressing to bind ingredients. Refrigerate overnight. This will last 6-7 days. Spread on pita chips or in pita pockets.

Medjool Dates Stuffed with Mascarpone Cheese

These taste like pumpkin pie with whipped cream, really dreamy tasting if you get good Medjool dates.

Allow 2 per person. Cut the date and remove the seed and fill the date with the Mascarpone. Friends will really think you are a gourmet chef when they bite into one of these delights.

Before Trip:

- Make wild rice tuna salad before trip and put in MSB, or make it on the trip. If you opt to make it on the trip, make it the day before you consume it.
- Buy dates, if you can find the Medjool dates which are moist, rich in flavor, and plump, you won't be disappointed and neither will your friends or family. Buy pita chips or bread, put in ZLB.

On Trip:

- Fill pita bread with tuna or spread on pita chips.
- Fill and set out dates and power bars.

Curry Almond Spread

Makes approximately 2 cups.

16-oz. cream cheese, slightly softened
1 cup chopped chutney, I use Major Grey's Mango chutney
2 t curry powder
1/2 t dry mustard or 1 1/2 t any good mustard you have on hand
3/4 cup sliced, toasted (in a toaster oven or regular oven) almonds
crackers, your favorite

Combine cheese, chutney, curry, and mustard. Blend well. When ready to serve add the toasted almonds. You can also put this in a bowl and sprinkle the almonds on top. This is very easy to make on a trip. You can toast your almonds at home and put in a ZLB. This will keep refrigerated about 6-7 days.

Turkey Tortilla Casserole

For you conscientious diet types (not me) this is actually a low-fat, low-cholesterol recipe, especially if you use yogurt instead of the sour cream.

Serves 8.

1 t olive oil
1 small onion, minced
2 cloves garlic, minced
1 lb ground turkey, or any other lean meat
2 T chili powder
1 t ground cumin
2 t dried oregano

1 T white vinegar
1 15-oz. canned black beans,
drained and rinsed twice
1 16-oz. jar mild, medium, or hot salsa
3/4 cup chicken broth
6 flour tortillas
3/4 cup grated Monterey Jack cheese
1/3 cup yogurt or sour cream

Meat Mixture:

Heat olive oil in skillet and sauté onion and garlic about 5 minutes. Add turkey, chili powder, cumin, oregano, and vinegar. Cook until turkey is no longer pink. If cooler space permits you can add the beans at this point. Cool and put in MSB and freeze. Put rest of ingredients in ZLB.

On the trip combine the salsa and chicken broth. Spread a thin layer in the bottom of a 10-inch DO. Top with half of the tortillas , half of the turkey bean mixture, and half of the salsa mixture. Repeat the layers and sprinkle with the cheese. Bake at 325° for 30-45 minutes. Top each serving with a little of the yogurt or sour cream.

Green Salad with Toasted Pepitas and Pecans

Makes 2 1/2 cups.

1 1/2 cup roasted pumpkin seeds   1 cup whole pecans
1 1/2 to 2 T butter, melted   salt to taste
For a spicy variation add garlic salt and cayenne pepper to taste.

Preheat oven to 350°. Place all seeds and nuts in a bowl and pour melted butter over all. Add salt and any other spices and mix. Spread all seeds and nuts on a cookie sheet. Bake 20 minutes stirring several times. If they begin to pop all over your oven, turn down the heat and bake a little longer until toasted. Cool and store in a tightly covered container. You can make these up several days before your trip.

Serve with iceberg lettuce, it lasts longer, and sprinkle with grated Parmesan cheese and ranch dressing.

Brown Sugar Orange Shortbread People

Makes 6 dozen cookies.

1/2 cup firmly packed light brown sugar   4 T orange zest (2-3 oranges)
2 sticks unsalted butter, cut into 16 equal parts, softened   2 1/2 cup unbleached flour
1 T orange juice   1/8 t salt

Mix sugar, butter, and orange juice until creamy. Add orange zest and blend. Stir in flour and salt and mix well. Wrap dough well in plastic wrap and refrigerate overnight. Preheat oven to 300°. Divide dough into three equal portions, put two of the portions in the refrigerator and work on the remaining one. On a lightly floured surface, roll the dough to a uniform 1/4-inch thickness. Use assorted, fun, floured cookie cutters to cut out the cookies and place them about 1 1/2 inches apart on ungreased baking sheets. Repeat with rest of dough. Bake cookies in center of preheated oven until firm but not dry, 20-25 minutes. Place cookies on wire rack to cool. Decorate as desired. I leave mine plain for raft trips, but decorate for parties. It's also fun to make shapes that are associated with the people on your raft trips. It makes for a nice surprise at the end of your meal. These can be made 2-3 weeks before trip and frozen in a ZLB.

Before Trip:

- Option of making curry almond spread.
- Make meat mixture for turkey tortilla casserole.
- Make pepitas and pecans.
- Make cookies.

On Trip:

- Make sure meat is defrosted the day before you make the turkey casserole.
- Make curry almond spread if you haven't already, set it out with your crackers.
- Get coals ready for casserole.
- Follow recipe for turkey casserole and begin baking.
- Make salad.

Menu Six
Days 5 - 12

Breakfast

Apple Walnut Oatmeal

Toast and Jams

Lunch

Marinated Lentil Salad

Spicy Oyster Crackers

Candy, Candy, Candy

Dinner

Celery Sticks with Herb Boursin Cheese

Beef Stew and Biscuits

Orange Slices with Grand Marnier

Pinot Noir, Cabernet Sauvignon, or Merlot

Apple Walnut Oatmeal

Serves 6.

2 cups uncooked oats, regular or quick cooking
3 small apples, cored and finely chopped
6 T toasted chopped walnuts

9 T maple syrup or brown sugar
dash of cinnamon

Cook oats according to package directions. Stir in apple, walnuts, maple syrup or brown sugar, and cinnamon; let stand covered for three minutes. Serve with milk or cream.

Toast and Jams

Use your favorite bread for toast. Pepperidge Farm is good and lasts a long time. I would allow at least two slices per person. Don't forget the butter and several fancy jams packaged in plastic containers.

Put a plain piece of bread on the grill of your gas stove, on a very low flame, just until slightly brown and then flip to the other side. Keep a close eye on this so you don't end up with blackened toast. You can also do this in a skillet with a little butter. Keep toast warm by wrapping in foil and setting near a flame. Also, if you feel energetic in the morning you can start some coals and put your bread directly on the grill and keep warm in a DO. You can also buy a camp stove toaster which will toast 4 slices of bread at once. They are cheap and fold up compactly for storage.

Before Trip:

- ZLB and label oatmeal.
- Buy apples the day before trip, wash and dry them.
- Toast, chop, and ZLB walnuts.
- Make sure maple syrup or brown sugar is in a plastic container.
- Put cinnamon in ZLB.
- Buy bread the day before trip and transfer to ZLB.
- Put butter and jams in plastic containers.

On Trip:

- Start coals if grilling bread.
- Make oatmeal.
- Make toast.
- Set everything out for a rib-sticking breakfast.

Marinated Lentil Salad

Serves 6.
This dish is very high in protein.

2/3 lb dried lentils	2 cloves garlic, pressed
1 large onion, finely chopped	1 large bay leaf
salt & pepper to taste	2 quarts of water
pinch of cayenne pepper	3 T wine vinegar
4 T olive oil	1 T lemon juice

Dressing:

1/4 cup onion, finely chopped	3-4 T olive oil
2/3 cup fresh parsley, chopped	juice of 1 lemon
salt & pepper to taste	

Garnish with stuffed olives and tomato wedges or sliced Napa or other cabbage. This should be made in advance and put in MSB. It will last two weeks in the cooler.

For lentils: soak overnight and drain. In a large pot, sauté the chopped onion in 2 T of the olive oil. Add the salt and pepper, flakes of cayenne pepper, garlic, bay leaf, the water, and the lentils. Simmer 1 1/2 – 2 hours. When the lentils are tender, drain and lightly rinse them. Let cool. Add 2 T of olive oil, the vinegar and the lemon juice, and set aside overnight.

For the dressing: combine the first 3 ingredients. Then add the olive oil, bit by bit, beating continuously until the dressing thickens. Then add the lemon juice, beat again, and pour over the lentils, mixing it in. Chill well. Pile lentils on a platter and add the garnishes.

Spicy Oyster Crackers

Makes 4 cups.

1/2 cup vegetable oil	dash cayenne pepper
1 package ranch dressing mix	dash lemon pepper (opt.)
1 t garlic powder	1 12-oz. package oyster crackers, large or small
1 t dill weed	

Mix all ingredients except crackers in a ZLB. Add crackers and shake well. Let stand two hours, shaking frequently. These can be kept in the freezer and may be served without thawing. Store them in a cool place. I find these addicting once I start munching on them.

Celery Sticks with Herb Boursin Cheese

Serves 6.

6 large stalks of celery washed and cut into 2-inch pieces crosswise
2 6-oz. packages of Herb Boursin Cheese, or any soft cheese

Prepare celery and spread cheese onto celery and serve. You can prepare celery before trip and put in ZLB or do it on your trip. Be sure and put packages of cheese in ZLB.

Beef Stew and Biscuits

Serves 6.

1 1/2 lbs of beef stew meat	1 14-oz. can diced tomatoes
1/2 cup celery, coarsely chopped	2 medium carrots, sliced
2 medium potatoes, cubed	1 1/2 medium onions, chopped
1 cup peas or green beans, fresh or frozen	2 T quick-cooking tapioca
1 beef or vegetable bouillon cube	1/2 t salt (opt.)
1/2 t sugar or maple syrup	freshly ground black pepper
1/4 t ground thyme	1/4 t rosemary leaves
1/4 t ground marjoram	1/4 cup fresh parsley, chopped
1/4 to 1/2 cup red wine	

Combine all ingredients in a 3-quart casserole. Cover and cook 3-5 hours at 325°. After two hours, stir well; continue cooking. Remove from oven, let cool completely. Put in MSB. The beauty of this dish is it is easy, you can make it ahead of time, freeze it, and it tastes delicious. If the stew is too thick, add more wine or water to whatever consistency you like your stew. You can also make this in a crock pot if you have a really large one.

On the trip, place the stew in a large DO on your stove top and heat through. Then do the topping.

Topping:

Buy Pillsbury biscuits in the refrigerator section of your grocery. I try to get at least a package of eight whole wheat biscuits. After opening rolls, separate and place on top of hot stew, put lid back on, place coals mainly on top, and bake 10-15 minutes more, until browned. Serve with a biscuit on top of each person's stew.

Orange Slices with Grand Marnier

Serves 6.

6 small naval oranges
1/4 to 1/2 cup Grand Marnier

Peel oranges and slice crosswise. Place on a serving platter and sprinkle Grand Marnier on top and let sit several minutes and serve. You can also use cognac. It's easy and light after the beef stew.

Before Trip:

- Cut celery into sticks.
- Make stew and get biscuits.
- Buy oranges and Grand Marnier.

On Trip:

- Start charcoal.
- Prepare celery sticks with cheese.
- Heat stew, then bake with biscuits.
- Prepare oranges.

Menu Seven

Days 5 - 12

Breakfast

Light and Fluffy Pancakes with Maple Syrup

Bacon

Orange Slices

Lunch

Garbanzo Salad

Assortment of Crackers

Dried Apricots and Pears

Dinner

Festive Nut and Fruit Mix

Mozzarella Crab Supreme

Colorful Salad

Orange Rum Cake

Sauvignon Blanc, Chardonnay

Light and Fluffy Pancakes

Serves 4-6.
These have a good flavor and texture.

2 cups of white flour	1/2 cup milk (more if batter is too thick)
4 t sugar	2 large eggs (powdered or fresh)
1 t salt	4 T unsalted butter, melted
1 t baking powder	vegetable oil for griddle
1/2 t baking soda	pure maple syrup
1 1/2 cup buttermilk (powdered is good)	

Mix dry ingredients in bowl. Pour buttermilk and milk into ta small bowl, beat in egg, and add this to dry ingredients and slightly mix. Add melted butter and blend. Do not over mix. Pancake batter should be a little lumpy. Meanwhile, heat griddle or large skillet over medium high heat. Spread a tablespoon of oil on griddle with spatula. When oil sizzles, pour batter onto griddle, about 1/8 cup to 1/4 cup at a time. When pancake bottoms are brown and top surface starts to bubble, 2 to 3 minutes, flip cakes and cook until remaining side has browned, 1 to 2 minutes longer. Re-oil griddle if necessary and repeat for next batch of pancakes. Serve with syrup.

Options:

Blueberry Pancakes.
You can add dried blueberries to your batter or drop fresh ones on top of each cooking pancake. I have actually found dried blueberries that taste just about as good as fresh in these pancakes.

Whole Wheat Pancakes
Follow recipe substituting 1 cup whole wheat flour for 1 cup of the white flour.

Toasted Pecan Pancakes
Toast your pecans or your favorite nut at home in a toaster oven or dry skillet shaking pan frequently until nuts are slightly brown and fragrant, 3-5 minutes. Chop nuts medium fine and add to batter or drop on top of each cooking pancake. Nuts keep longer in a ZLB in the freezer roasted or unroasted.

Before Trip:

- Put all dry ingredients in ZLB.
- Put butter in ZLB.
- Put vegetable oil in plastic bottle.
- Don't forget the canned bacon and oranges.
- Put maple syrup in a plastic bottle.

On Trip:

- Fry up bacon.
- Peel and slice oranges crosswise. Put on a platter, or just set out unpeeled oranges in a bowl.
- Mix up pancakes, don't forget to add the liquid if you're using all powdered ingredients.
- Set out syrup and dig in.

Garbanzo Salad

1/2 cup olive oil	1/4-1/2 cup dark raisins
1/2 cup minced onions	2 1-lb cans garbanzo beans, drained and rinsed
1 T dried thyme	1/2 t salt
1/2 cup chopped red bell pepper	1/2 cup white vinegar
1/2 cup chopped yellow bell pepper	

Cook in skillet olive oil, onion, and thyme until tender, 5-10 minutes. Add peppers and cook 1 minute. Add raisins and garbanzo beans and cook 3 minutes. Do not overcook. Season with salt, transfer to bowl, and pour vinegar over hot mixture. Let cool and refrigerate for 24 hours. It keeps well in the fridge for 3-4 days. This is a delicious and easy salad to prepare a few days before you are ready to eat it.

Before Trip:

- Pack crackers.
- Put dried fruit in ZLB.
- Pack beans.
- Wash, dry and pack bell peppers.
- Pack 1 small onion.
- Put thyme and salt in ZLB.
- Put olive oil in plastic container.
- Put vinegar in plastic container.
- Put raisins in ZLB.

On Trip:

- Prepare garbanzo salad 1 or 2 days before you eat it.

Festive Nut and Fruit Mix

Serves 8.

> 8-oz. salted roasted cashews
> 8-oz. pepitas or roasted pumpkin seeds
> 1/3 lb dried cranberries or dried cherries

Combine all in a clear bowl and toss to combine. It looks very festive when served in a clear container, even a wine glass.

Mozzarella Crab Supreme

Serves 4-6.

1/4 cup butter
1/2 cup red onion, chopped
1/3 cup green bell pepper, chopped
1/4 cup flour
1/2 t salt
1/4 t pepper

2 cups milk
3/4 cup grated mozzarella cheese
8-oz. package of canned crabmeat, flaked
1/2 can chopped water chestnuts (opt.)
8-oz. spaghetti, cooked

Melt butter in saucepan. Sauté onions and green peppers in butter. Add flour, salt, and pepper. Stir over low heat until combined. Remove from heat. Add milk and blend well. Return to heat. Bring mixture to a boil stirring constantly. Boil 1 minute. Add cheese and melt until combined. Add crabmeat and chestnuts. Heat thoroughly. Serve over cooked spaghetti. Also good over toasted English muffins for brunch.

Colorful Salad

Serves 4.

> 1 14-oz. can drained corn
> 1/2 cup shredded carrots
> 2 cups red baby new potatoes, cooked in boiling water until slightly soft
> when pierced by a fork or knife, sliced in half
> salt and pepper to taste
> 1 T dill

Empty all ingredients into a large bowl, stir, and serve.

Orange Rum Cake

Serves 8-10.
I have been making this golden oldie cake since 1973. It was a huge hit on our last Middle Fork trip.

1 cup (2 sticks) soft butter
2 cups sugar
2 eggs (powdered is fine)
2 1/2 cups sifted flour
1 t baking soda

2 t baking powder
1/2 t salt
1 cup buttermilk (powdered works well)
grated rind of 2 large oranges and 1 lemon
1 cup walnuts

Topping:

Juice of 2 large oranges and 1 lemon
1 cup sugar
2 T rum, or 1 T each rum and Grand Marnier
Boil fruit juices and sugar together for 3 minutes. Add rum and stir.

Cream together butter and sugar. Add eggs and mix. Sift flour, baking soda, baking powder, and salt into mixture and stir. Add buttermilk and grated rinds, mix. Add walnuts and stir. I make this in my tube pan at home and in a 10-inch DO on the river. Be sure your pan is lightly greased and floured before pouring in your batter. Bake at 350° for 1 hour at home and around 40-50 minutes on the river. Let it sit for 5 minutes. At home you can remove it from the pan and baste with the fruit mixture. On the river, just pour the juices over the cake in the DO. Don't forget to add water if you are using powdered eggs or buttermilk, or you may end up being the brunt of many a joke.

Before Trip:

- Make nut and fruit mix.
- Pack ingredients for entire dinner.

On Trip:

- Prepare cake.
- Make salad.
- Prepare crab supreme.

Menu Eight
Days 5 - 12

Breakfast

Tex-Mex Migas with Salsa and Soft Tortillas

Refried Black Beans

Lunch

Curried Tuna Salad with Apples and Currants

Wheat or Cocktail Bread

Mixed Nuts

Dinner

Vegetables with Cheese Dip

Spicy Sausage and Lentil Stew

Corn Bread

Orange with Limoncello

Orange Shortbread Cookies

Merlot

Tex-Mex Migas with Salsa
and Soft Tortillas

Serves 4.

> 4 T butter or oil
> 8 eggs, beaten
> 4 T onions or scallions, chopped
> 4 T Monterey Jack cheese, grated
> 4 T Longhorn cheese or a sharp cheddar cheese, grated
> 4 T green chile peppers. I use Hatch chiles, roasted, peeled, seeded and chopped
> 2 handfuls of tortilla chips, crumbled
> salsa
> soft flour tortillas

Melt butter in a skillet over medium heat. Add the eggs, onions and cheeses, and chile peppers. Scramble until almost cooked. Add the chips and mix them in. Serve with your favorite salsa and warm flour tortillas.

Refried Black Beans

Buy canned or refer to Menu 3, Days 1-4. I love black beans so I've included them in several recipes. Hope y'all don't mind.

Before Trip:

- Put butter in ZLB.
- Put eggs in plastic container.
- Put onions in ZLB.
- Put cheeses in ZLB. Put chile peppers in ZLB.
- Put tortilla chips in ZLB.
- Don't forget the beans.
- Put soft tortillas in a ZLB.
- Put your salsa in a plastic container.

On Trip:

- Make sure your refried beans are thawed in advance.
- Warm tortillas wrapped in foil over coals on a grill, on a pot of steaming water, or in a dry skillet on a low flame.
- Heat refried beans in a skillet or pot.
- Whip up the migas and you are set to serve a Tex-Mex breakfast.

Curried Tuna Salad
with Apples and Currants

Makes 4 sandwiches.

2 6-oz. cans solid white tuna in water	2 T juice from one lemon
1/2 t salt	1/2 cup or less of mayonnaise
1/4 t ground black pepper	1 T curry powder
1 small rib of celery, minced	
1 T minced red onion	1/4 t Dijon mustard
1 medium firm apple, cut into 1/4-inch pieces	2 T fresh basil leaves, or 1 T dry basil leaves
1/4 cup or less currants	(fresh basil really makes it more tasty)

Add drained tuna to a bowl and break down clumps with a fork. Add salt, pepper, celery, onion, apple, currants, and stir. Mix lemon juice, mayonnaise, curry powder, mustard, and basil leaves in separate bowl. Then add all these ingredients to the tuna and mix. This can be made 1 or 2 days in advance. It is also nice to serve as open-faced sandwiches on a variety of cocktail breads.

Before Trip:

- Pack all ingredients in ZLB.
- Be sure to wash apple.
- Peel onion before placing in ZLB.
- Clean celery and pat dry to put in ZLB.
- Pack cans of tuna.
- Wash basil, pat dry, put in ZLB.
- Take mixed nuts.

On Trip: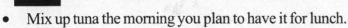

- Mix up tuna the morning you plan to have it for lunch.

Vegetables with Cheese Dip

Makes about 1 cup.

1 8-oz. package cream cheese, softened
1 t grated onion
3 T catsup
salt to taste

1/2 t dry mustard
1/4 t cayenne
dash Worcestershire sauce
2-4 T cream or milk
vegetables, cut up

Combine all ingredients except veggies in a mixer or by hand. This dip is best prepared the day before but will last 6-7 days if refrigerated. Serve with any raw vegetables.

Spicy Sausage and Lentil Stew

Serves 10.

1 lb dry or canned lentils
1 small bay leaf
1 t salt
1/2 t each of garlic salt, dry mustard, ground cinnamon, ground cloves,
ground ginger, ground nutmeg, dried savory, and dried thyme, crushed
8-oz. of your favorite sausage, I use Polish, German, or a good
Texas sausage, cut in 1/2-inch chunks or slices
2 medium onions, sliced
2 cups tomato juice. I mix 1 6-oz. can tomato paste or 1 8-oz. can tomato sauce
and water to make 2 cups. The paste gives a little more tomato flavor. I use which ever
one I have on hand in my pantry.
1 15-oz. can (2 cups) tomato sauce
3 T molasses

If using canned lentils skip this step. In a DO or large pot combine lentils, 5 cups water, and seasonings. Bring to boil, reduce heat, and simmer, covered, for 35 minutes.

In a skillet cook sausage and onion till meat is lightly browned. Add to stew with remaining ingredients. Simmer, covered, 15 minutes.

This is so easy and delicious. I've made this for years and people love it. You can add or delete portions of spices depending on how much you prefer. I usually make this a few days in advance so that the spices can really mellow. This can also be frozen in an MSB.

Corn Bread

Serves 6.

3/4 cup cornmeal
1 cup white flour
1/4 cup sugar
3 t baking powder
3/4 t salt

Add to above:

1 cup milk
1 egg
3 T butter, melted by putting butter into an 8 x 8 square glass baking dish in your oven at home or a 10-inch DO

Melt the butter while mixing the above ingredients, it should remain lumpy NOT smooth. Don't over mix! Add melted butter to batter and stir a few times. Pour batter into hot dish or DO. Bake at 400° for about 20 minutes or until a toothpick inserted in center comes out clean.

This is my Mom's recipe and I've adjusted it a little to my taste by adding less sugar. The amazing thing about this recipe is that it is so simple and good that you will want to whip it up all the time, like we do at home.

Limoncello

Makes 3 quarts.

This is really nice on the oranges, very refreshing. It also makes a nice after dinner drink in small doses, as well as great gifts, but you will need to start several months in advance. This drink is served in many restaurants in Italy and can be purchased at a liquor store.

15 thick-skinned lemons
2 750-ml bottles of 100 proof Vodka

4 cups of sugar
5 cups of water

To begin, secure a large glass jar (4 quarts) with a lid. Wash the lemons well. Pat dry and remove the zest. If you do get some of the pith (white part of lemon) with the zest, carefully scrape it away with the tip of a knife. Fill the jar with one bottle of the vodka and, as you remove the zest, add it to the jar. After combining the vodka and lemon zest, cover the jar and store it at room temperature in a dark cabinet or cupboard. After about 40 days, combine the sugar and water in a saucepan, bring it to a boil, and cook until thickened, about 5 minutes. Let the syrup cool before adding it to the Limoncello mixture, along with the other bottle of vodka. Cover and return to the cupboard for another 40 days. Strain the Limoncello into bottles and discard the lemon zest. You can store the bottles in a cupboard, but always keep one in the freezer so it's icy cold when you're ready to drink it. On a raft trip serve as a liqueur, cold if possible.

Alternate Liqueurs:
Grand Marnier • Mandarine Napoleon • Cointreau

Orange Shortbread Cookies

Makes 6 dozen cookies.
I like to keep dough in my freezer in case the neighborhood kids drop by. These can also be dipped in warm chocolate and left to harden on a cookie rack. Yummy.

2 cups of pecans, roasted first, then ground	1 t vanilla
3 sticks butter, softened	3 cups flour
1/2 cup sugar	zest of 1 orange
1/2 cup powdered sugar	

Roast pecans in a toaster oven for 1 to 2 minutes. Mix butter and sugars. Add vanilla and zest. Add flour and nuts, mix well. Form dough into a log shape on foil about 1 to 1 1/2 inches in diameter. Roll up and twist ends of foil to compact dough. Refrigerate dough until firm enough to slice. Slice 1/8-1/4-inch slices and bake at 350° on nonstick cookie sheet for 12 minutes. Both baked cookies and dough freeze well.

Before Trip:

- Mix cheese dip and put in a plastic container or bring ingredients in separate containers. Put cleaned veggies in ZLB.
- Make sausage and lentil stew and put in MSB. Freeze until trip. Or bring ingredients in separate containers and make on trip.
- Measure and put dry ingredients for cornbread in ZLB. Dried milk and eggs can go with dry ingredients, otherwise put milk in plastic bottle and eggs in a another plastic bottle. Put butter in ZLB.
- Make or buy Limoncello.
- Make shortbread cookies, put in ZLB and freeze until trip.

On Trip:

- Set out dip and veggies.
- Start coals for cornbread.
- Make or warm up stew.
- Make cornbread.
- Slice oranges and let macerate in Limoncello. Serve with a platter of the shortbread cookies. You can also drink the Limoncello, very tasty when it is cold.

Menu Nine

Days 5 - 12

Breakfast

Apple Whole Wheat Pancakes with Maple Syrup

Grilled Fruit Kabobs

Lunch

Ratatouille Caviar with Pita Bread

Kosher Sliced Dill Pickles

Sesame Seed Cookies

Dinner

Wonton Soup

Mixed Vegetable Curry

Toasted Almonds with Cayenne and Cumin Butter

Beet Yogurt Salad

Curried Garbanzo Beans

Pistachio Halva

Zinfandel or Pinot Gris

Apple Whole Wheat Pancakes

Serves 4-6.

4 T (1/2 stick) butter
2 eggs, beaten, or powdered eggs
1/4 cup maple syrup or brown sugar
1/4 cup water
3/4 cup apple juice (canned)
1 t vanilla
2 cups whole wheat flour

1 T powdered milk
1/2 t cinnamon
1 t baking soda
1 t baking powder
1/8 t salt
1-2 red apples, finely chopped or grated

Melt butter, set aside. Chop or grate apples, set aside. Mix eggs and maple syrup together, add melted butter, water, apple juice, and vanilla. Sift dry ingredients and mix lightly into liquid. Batter should be lumpy. Add chopped apples and stir. Serve with additional maple syrup.

Grilled Fruit Kabobs

This will make your breakfast a little more interesting and tasty, especially good on a layover day. you can use just about any fruit in season. Some suggestions would be oranges (with peels left on) cut in eighths, figs, apricots, melons, bananas, canned or fresh pineapples, peaches, papayas, nectarines, or plums.

Brush fruit with a little melted butter and brown sugar/maple syrup before grilling, or try lemon juice, balsamic or flavored vinegars to enhance the fruit's natural sweetness. If using wooden skewers, soak in water 5-10 minutes so they don't catch fire. Wipe down skewers with olive oil before grilling so food can be slipped off more easily. Also use 2 skewers per kabob, slightly apart, so the fruit will stay on better. Have fun and be experimental. Cut up a selection of fruit and let everyone do his/her own skewer. It's fun and will help wake people up for the day to come.

Before Trip:

- Put all dry ingredients in ZLB.
- Put butter in ZLB.
- Vanilla in small plastic bottle.
- Maple syrup in a plastic bottle.
- Don't forget canned apple juice.
- Buy wooden skewers.
- Buy 1/4 lb of fruit per person.
- Take a little extra maple syrup or brown sugar, lemon juice or balsamic vinegar for fruit kabobs.

On Trip:

- Start coals for kabobs.
- Get fruit and skewers ready for kabobs.
- Lay fruit out on a platter so people can start making their own kabobs.
- Prepare pancake batter and make pancakes.
- Make the pancakes.

Ratatouille Caviar
with Pita Bread

Makes 5 cups.
Ratatouille is a Mediterranean vegetable dish. It is worth making in quantity because of its many uses in omelets, crepes, soups, stews, pastas, pancakes, salads, and sandwiches. It also freezes well and can last at least ten days refrigerated and can be served cold or reheated. In this recipe, it is an ingredient in the caviar.

Ratatouille Caviar

Makes about 2 cups.

3/4 cup fresh parsley leaves, loosely packed, minced
1 small clove garlic, peeled and minced
3/4 cup pitted black olives, drained
1 t fresh lemon juice
1/4 t salt

2 T onion, chopped
1 cup Ratatouille, drained (recipe below)
1/3 cup mayonnaise
1/2 t dried dill weed

You can make this in a food processor by adding the parsley first and adding all other ingredients in the order listed. Or you can finely mince everything by hand. Either way this is very good in pita bread or on any bread.

Ratatouille

2/3 cup fresh parsley leaves, loosely packed, minced
2 large cloves garlic, peeled and chopped
1/2 lb tomatoes (about 2 medium) peeled, seeded
and quartered, or canned plum tomatoes,
drained, coarsely chopped
1 medium eggplant (about 1 1/4 lb), unpeeled, cubed
3 medium zucchini (about 1 lb), sliced 1/4-inch thick
1 T salt
1/4 cup olive oil
1 t ground coriander

1 t crushed dried thyme
2 large onions (about 1/2 lb),
peeled, halved and sliced 1/4 inch
2 small green bell peppers (about 6-oz.),
cut in half and sliced 1/4 inch
3 T tomato paste and 9 T water,
mixed together
pinch of sugar
1 1/2 t dried basil
salt and fresh ground pepper to taste

Transfer zucchini and eggplant to a colander in the sink. Sprinkle them with the salt, toss with your fingers. Let stand 30 minutes to let excess moisture exude and to release some of the bitterness of the eggplant. Pat vegetables dry with paper towels. Heat the olive oil in a 14-inch skillet. Sauté the onions and garlic. Add tomato paste and water. Add the coriander, thyme, pinch of sugar, dried basil and stir. Add tomatoes, eggplant, zucchini, bell peppers and simmer until the liquid is somewhat evaporated and it looks like a sauce. Add salt and pepper, cool and refrigerate or freeze.

Sesame Seed Cookies

Makes about 2 dozen cookies.
These are crisp, mildly flavored cookies to which one can easily become addicted.

2 cups flour	1 large egg
3/4 cup sugar	2 T cold water
1 t baking powder	water for brushing
1/2 cup butter (or butter flavored Crisco), at room temperature	1/3 cup sesame seeds

Process first 6 ingredients with the metal blade of a food processor until the mixture forms a ball, about 30 seconds. Add additional water by the teaspoon if the mixture does not form a ball, process about 10 more seconds. Flatten the mixture into a 1-inch thick disc, wrap in plastic wrap and refrigerate for 1 hour. Preheat oven to 375°. Put plastic wrap and dough in middle of cookie sheet and unwrap. Keep plastic wrap on cookie sheet with dough on top and begin rolling the dough on the plastic (this eliminates the need to use additional flour) to a 15 x 10-inch rectangle about 1/4-inch thick. Brush the dough with water. Sprinkle the sesame seeds on the dough and spread them evenly over the surface with your hands. Press down lightly to secure the seeds. Cut out the cookies with a 3-inch cookie cutter, or you can cut the dough with a knife into squares or rectangles. Slide the plastic off the cookie sheet and line the sheet with parchment paper. Use a knife to carefully remove cookies from the plastic wrap onto the parchment paper, seed side up. The scraps can be baked for informal munching. Bake in the center of the preheated oven until lightly browned and firm to the touch, about 15 to 20 minutes.

Before Trip:

- Make Ratatouille caviar and freeze in ZLB.
- Make sesame seed cookies and freeze in ZLB.

On Trip:

- Set everything out and chow down.

152

Wonton Soup

Buy this in packages at the grocery store.

Mixed Vegetable Curry

with Cayenne and Cumin Butter Toasted Almonds

Makes 4 servings.

3 T vegetable oil
1 onion, sliced
1 t ground cumin
1 t chili powder
2 t ground coriander
1 t ground turmeric
8 oz. potatoes, diced

6 oz. zucchini
4 oz. green beans, sliced
6 oz. carrots, diced
1 14.5-oz. can diced tomatoes
1/2 to 3/4 cup hot vegetable stock, canned, or make your own.
canned onion rings for garnish (opt.).

Heat oil in large saucepan, add onion and cook 5 minutes until softened. Stir in spices; cook 2 min. Add potatoes, zucchini, green beans, and carrots, tossing them with spices until coated. Add tomatoes, stock and cover. Bring to a boil, reduce heat and simmer 10 to 12 minutes or until vegetables are just tender but a little crunchy. Serve hot with onion rings on top with any type of cooked noodles underneath, or without the noodles. You can use any mixture of vegetables to make a total of 1 1/2 lbs, such as turnips, cauliflower, eggplant, parsnips or leeks. All are good.

Toasted Almonds

with Cayenne and Cumin Butter

Use this recipe over the veggie curry dish.

1 lb slivered almonds
1/4-1/2 t cayenne

1 T cumin
2 T butter

Melt butter over low heat in a large skillet. Add cayenne and cumin, stir. Add almonds, stirring until almonds are coated and golden brown. Cool and freeze, or refrigerate until ready to eat.

Beet Yogurt Salad

Makes 4-6 servings.

6 cooked small beets
1 cup plain yogurt
1 t sugar
salt and red pepper to taste (cayenne, or I use Chimayo chile powder from New Mexico.)

You can use canned beets, but fresh beets are much better and crisper. Cook beets ahead of time and store in a ZLB in refrigerator before your trip. Stir sugar, salt and pepper into yogurt about 30 minutes before adding to beets. Cut cold beets into 1/8-inch thick slices and arrange on a serving plate. Keep all in a cooler until ready to assemble. Pour yogurt over beets when ready to serve.

Curried Garbanzo Beans

Serves 4.

1 cup dried garbanzo beans, or
1 15-oz. can garbanzo beans (chick peas)
salt to taste
2 T vegetable oil
1 small onion, finely chopped
1 (1-inch) piece fresh ginger root, grated

2 clove garlic, crushed
1/2 t ground turmeric
1 t ground cumin
1 t Garam Masala (recipe below)
1/2 t chili powder (your favorite)
2 T chopped cilantro (opt.)

For dried garbanzo beans:
Rinse beans, put in a cooking pot, cover with cold water and soak overnight. Drain beans, add 2 cups of cold water and salt. Boil 10 min., reduce heat and simmer 1 hour, partially covered.

In a separate skillet, heat oil, add onion, cook about 8 minutes, until soft and golden brown. Add ginger root, garlic, turmeric, cumin, Garam Masala, and chili powder; cook 1 minute. Stir in beans and their cooking water and bring to a boil. Cover and simmer 20 minutes, 10 minutes if using canned garbanzo beans, until beans are very tender, but still whole. Serve hot, sprinkled with chopped cilantro.

Garam Masala

1 T plus 1 t cardamom seeds
2 (3-inch) cinnamon sticks, crushed
2 t whole cloves

1 T plus 1 t black peppercorns
3 T cumin seeds
3 T coriander seeds

Heat all spices in a heavy skillet and dry roast over medium heat 5 to 10 minutes, until browned, stirring constantly. Cool completely, then grind to a fine powder in a coffee grinder or with a mortar and pestle. Store in an airtight jar up to 2 months. This is used in many Indian recipes and in making hot tea. It's wonderful stuff.

Pistachio Halva

This is delicate and needs to be refrigerated.

1 1/4 cups shelled pistachios	1/2 cup sugar
1 cup boiling water	1 1/2 T butter or ghee
2 T milk	1 t vanilla

Put pistachios in a bowl, top with boiling water and soak 30 minutes. Grease and line an 8-inch square pan with waxed paper. Drain pistachios thoroughly and put in a blender or food processor fitted with the metal blade. Add milk and process until finely chopped, scraping mixture down from sides once or twice. Stir in sugar. Heat a large non-stick skillet, add butter and melt over medium-low heat. Add nut paste and cook about 15 minutes, stirring constantly, until mixture is very thick. Stir in vanilla, then spoon into prepared pan and spread evenly. Cool completely, then cut into 20 squares with a sharp knife. This halva will keep 2 to 3 weeks covered in a refrigerator or cooler.

Before Trip:

- Combine spices in ZLB for each of the dishes.
- Make sure oil is in plastic container.
- Make curried garbanzo beans 1 to 2 days before trip and refrigerate in ZLB.
- Make Pistachio Halva and freeze in ZLB.

On Trip:

- Make curried vegetables.
- Put together beet salad.
- Set out curried garbanzo beans.
- Set out Pistachio Halva.

Menu Ten

Days 5 - 12

Breakfast

Baked Cinnamon Sugar Rolls

Selection of Cold Cereals with Milk

Fruit and Yogurt

Lunch

Moroccan Orzo Salad

Pita Chips

Baby Carrots

Smash Snacks

Dinner

Salsa and Chips

Black Bean and Goat Cheese Enchiladas

Spicy Rice

Guacamole

Pecan Pralines

Gars, Short for Margaritas

Baked Cinnamon Sugar Rolls

Serves 10.
These are really yummy, gooey, and smell great.

> 2 cans biscuits (I use Grand Whole Wheat, 8 in a can)
> 1/2 to 3/4 cup melted butter
> 10 T sugar and 1 t cinnamon, mixed together

Put in bottom of DO:

> 1 cup walnuts, chopped
> 3 T melted butter
> 2 T maple syrup

Variation 1

Remove biscuits from can, cut each biscuit in half and roll into a ball, dip in melted butter, then roll in cinnamon sugar mixture. Place in bottom of a 10-inch DO and bake 20-25 minutes at 375°.

Variation 2

You can also do this as a dinner bread, just dip biscuits in melted butter and then in grated Parmesan cheese. Adding herbs would also be nice. Omit the nuts/butter/syrup.

Before Trip:

- Butter in a ZLB.
- Sugar and cinnamon in a ZLB.
- Buy canned, dry, or carton milk.

On Trip:

- Start coals for biscuits.
- Bake rolls in DO.
- Cut up fruit of your choice and set out with yogurt.
- Set out cereals and milk.

Moroccan Orzo Salad

Serves 6.

1/2 lb orzo (pasta shaped like rice)	1/2 cup raisins
1/4 cup olive oil	1/4 cup sliced almonds (toasted in oven/toaster oven)
2 T lemon juice	2 T chopped roasted or raw red bell pepper
1/4 t cinnamon	1/4 cup diced sweet yellow onion (I like to sauté mine)
1/8 t ground cardamom	1/4 cup canned garbanzo beans, drained
1/8 t ground mace	salt to taste

Cook orzo in boiling water according to package directions. Drain, rinse with cold water and drain well. While pasta cooks, combine olive oil, lemon juice and spices in a serving bowl; whisk well. Stir in remaining ingredients, except the almonds, they should be added just before serving. Stir in drained pasta. This can be made on the river, or made and frozen ahead of time and kept in the cooler.

Smash Snacks

Makes about 4 dozen pieces.

2 1/2 cups thin pretzel sticks, broken into 1-inch pieces
2 1/4 cups uncooked oats (quick or old-fashioned)
1 cup raisins
1 cup dry roasted peanuts, or other roasted nuts
10-oz. package of peanut butter-flavored butterscotch chips or toffee chips
2 cups semisweet or bittersweet chocolate chips
3/4 cup honey

In a large bowl, add first 4 ingredients. Mix well. In a large saucepan, combine rest of ingredients stirring until chips are melted. Pour over oat mixture stirring until dry ingredients are well coated. Spread and smash mixture on to foil-lined cookie sheet, working mixture to edge of sheet. Place in refrigerator until firm. Break into pieces. Store tightly at room temperature. On a hot weather trip keep these in the cooler.

Before Trip:

- Cook orzo and freeze in ZLB, or cook on trip.
- Olive oil in plastic container.
- Lemon juice in plastic container.
- Spices combined in ZLB.
- Raisins & Almonds in seperate ZLB.
- Red pepper in ZLB in cooler. Onion in ZLB in cooler.
- Garbanzo beans in ZLB in cooler.
- Make smash snacks.

On Trip:

- Make orzo salad the day before or the day you serve it.
- Set everything else out to be eaten at lunch.

Black Bean and Goat Cheese Enchiladas

Serves 4.
This might seem a bit time consuming but is well worth the effort. The flavors and textures are wonderful to the palate.

1 1/2 cup chicken broth
8 or 10 tomatillos (husks removed), rinsed and chopped (or substitute green tomatoes, canned or fresh)
6 cloves of garlic, peeled
1 cup yellow onion, chopped
4 serrano chiles, stemmed and seeded
2 T fresh cilantro or parsley, chopped
2 cups cooked/canned black beans, see Menu 3, Days 1-4
8 T fresh mango or papaya, diced (in a real pinch you could use canned peaches, but be sure they are rinsed of the syrup they are packed in)

4 T onion
8 T corn kernels (opt.) fresh/canned
1/2 cup goat cheese
salt to taste
1/2 cup corn oil
8 corn tortillas
1 cup diced red bell peppers, opt. garnish

For salsa, in a medium-sized saucepan, cook 1 cup chicken broth, tomatillos, 4 cloves garlic, onion, and 2 serrano chiles over medium-high heat for 10 minutes, stirring frequently. Place mixture in blender with cilantro and puree until smooth. Set salsa aside. Mince remaining garlic and serrano chiles. In another saucepan, place black beans, remaining 1/2 cup chicken broth, minced garlic and chile, mango or papaya, 4 T onion, and corn. Bring to a boil and whisk in goat cheese, if using peaches add now and stir. Season with salt, remove from heat and keep warm with lid or foil on top. Heat oil in skillet until just smoking. Pass each tortilla through the oil to moisten and seal. Place between paper towels to drain. Place 1/4 cup of bean and goat cheese mixture down center of each tortilla. Roll tortillas and place, seam-side down, in 12-inch DO. Spoon 1/2 of salsa over tortillas, cover and bake just until heated through, about 20-25 minutes at 350°. Serve with rest of heated salsa and sprinkle red pepper on top.

Spicy Rice

Serves 6.

1 cup Texmati or Basmati rice
1 t oil
3 T dry roasted, unsalted cashew nuts
2 T fresh sugar peas, canned peas also work
1 T currants

1 t curry powder
1/2 t salt
1/4 t cinnamon
1/4 t nutmeg
2 cups water

Wash rice and drain well. Sauté a few minutes in oil. Add cashews, peas, and currants. Stir well, add spices and water, and stir again. Cover and bring to a boil, reduce heat, and simmer until all water is gone, about 30 to 40 minutes. You can also sprinkle the nuts on the rice after it is cooked.

Guacamole

Serves 6.

There are many variations on guacamole. This is my version which is very simple and very Tex-Mex. You can also take the short cut and buy pre-made guacamole. I don't add a lot to my guacamole because simple is best when it comes to avocados.

4 large avocados
juice of 1 to 2 limes

1-2 cloves of garlic
salt to taste
iceberg lettuce

Mash avocados but leave some lumps. Add lime, keep tasting so that it doesn't have too much lime. Peel the garlic. Mash the garlic with a pinch of salt (this makes it easier to mash), with the heel of your hand pressed upon the flat side of a sharp knife, or in a mortar and pestle. Add to avocado mixture and stir. Serve on top of iceberg lettuce.

Gars (Short For Margaritas)

For recipe, refer to Menu 5, Days 1-4.

Before Trip:

- Make salsa for enchiladas and freeze in ZLB.
- Make black beans minus the fruit and goat cheese, put in ZLB and freeze.
- Buy tortillas, can be frozen in ZLB.
- Corn oil in plastic container.
- Precook rice and freeze in ZLB, or make rice dish on trip.
- Cashews in ZLB.
- Rice spices in ZLB.
- Currants in ZLB.
- Buy canned or fresh peas (day before trip and put in ZLB in refrigerator).
- Buy pralines. Lammes Texas Chewie Pecan Pralines are excellent (www.lammes.com).
- Don't forget the lettuce.

On Trip:

- Make gars and set out salsa and chips.
- Heat coals.
- Make enchiladas and bake.
- Make rice.
- Make guacamole.
- Set out pralines.

Menu Eleven

Days 5 - 12

Breakfast

Chile Cheese Grits

Biscuits

Sliced Ham

Lunch

Garbanzo Bean and Potato Salad

Assorted Crackers

Seasonal Fresh Fruit

Dinner

Horsey D's Nuts and Seeds

Pineapple Marinated Chicken Kabobs with Grilled Vegetables

Mixed Rice with Pecans and Raisins

Yummy Brownies

Semillon/Gewurztraminer

Chile Cheese Grits

Serves 6-8.

3/4 cup white grits
3 cups water
3/4 t salt
1/2 cup butter
1/2 lb white cheddar cheese
1 t seasoned salt

1/2 t Worcestershire sauce
2 eggs, well beaten
1 4-oz. can chopped green chiles. I use freshly roasted Hatch chiles because of the great flavor they impart. I keep them chopped up in the freezer in an MSB for whenever I need them.
paprika or chili powder

Bring water to a boil. Add grits and salt. Cook over low heat 2-5 minutes, stirring occasionally. Add butter and cheese. Stir until melted. Add seasoned salt and Worcestershire sauce. Fold in eggs. Add chiles. Pour into a buttered 10-inch DO and bake 40-50 minutes or until done. Sprinkle with paprika or chili powder and serve. Note: If you want to make this at home, preheat your oven to 350° and follow the above directions.

Biscuits

Serves 8-10.

2 cans biscuits put into a slightly oiled 12-inch DO to bake 10-12 minutes
Serve with butter and jams.

Sliced Ham

Buy semi-thick slices of your favorite ham that has been pre-cooked, or a small canned ham that you can slice. Heat in a skillet on the stove with a 1/4 cup of water so the ham won't dry out. Or you can fry the ham with 1 or 2 T of oil. Start this when your grits are almost finished and when you start your biscuits baking. Keep ham warm by placing it in foil or a lid on the skillet.

Before Trip:

- Everything should be in a plastic container or ZLB.

On Trip:

- Start coals for grits and biscuits.
- Make grits and bake.
- Bake biscuits.
- Heat sliced ham.

Garbanzo Bean and Potato Salad

Serves 6.

1 T tamarind paste (Indian/Asian food store)
2 T hot water
2 T lime juice
2 T vegetable oil
1 t soy sauce
1/2 t salt
1/2 t ground cumin

1/4 t red pepper flakes
4 small scallions, trimmed and cut into 2-inch lengths
1 t finely chopped fresh coriander (cilantro), or parsley
1 lb small red potatoes, cooked, cut into cubes
1 can garbanzo beans (chick peas), drained
2 large hard-cooked eggs, peeled and sliced, for garnish

Soak the tamarind paste in hot water for 30 minutes. Mash paste with a fork, then strain through a sieve, pressing the mixture with the back of a spoon. Reserve liquid and discard the solids. Process or blend the tamarind liquid, lime juice, oil, soy sauce, salt, cumin, and pepper flakes about 10 seconds. Slice scallions. Add all this to the coriander, potatoes, and garbanzo beans. Toss to combine. Let sit for about one hour covered. Garnish with sliced eggs and serve. Doesn't have to be cold when serving.

Before Trip:

- Make dressing for salad, put in plastic container or MSB.
- Make hard boiled eggs, can also be made on trip.

On Trip:

- Cook potatoes.
- Chop coriander.
- Chop scallions.
- Drain garbanzo beans.
- Mix all ingredients and add dressing.
- Set out crackers.
- Set out fruit.

Horsey D's Nuts and Seeds

almonds

walnuts

soy nuts

sunflower seeds

pecans

cashews

sesame seeds

peanuts

onion powder

chili powder (your choice)

celery salt

soy sauce

oil

Mix nuts and seeds, add spices to taste. Add soy sauce and oil just to lightly coat nuts. Spread in roasting pan and roast at 350° in oven, stirring frequently until toasted, about 20 minutes.

Pineapple Marinated Chicken Kabobs

with Grilled Vegetables

Serves 6-8.

I've included two marinades here because I honestly could not decide which one I liked best. Try both and you be the judge. If making ahead of time, add 1/4 cup vodka or other liquor to help preserve it.

Marinade 1

4-5 large skinless, boneless chicken breasts

1/2 cup pineapple juice

1/2 cup soy sauce

1/2 cup canola/vegetable oil or melted butter

Mix all ingredients and let chicken marinate for 10 to 15 min.

Marinade 2

4-5 large skinless, boneless chicken breasts

2 t fresh ginger or 3 t powdered

1 T maple syrup or brown sugar

1 t dry mustard

1/4 cup canola/vegetable oil

1/2 cup pineapple juice

1 t garlic salt

1/2 t pepper

1/2 cup soy sauce

Place all ingredients in a sauce pan and simmer for five minutes. Let cool completely before pouring over chicken. Marinate 20-30 minutes or longer if you have more time.

For kabobs: Cube chicken into chunks and place on metal or wooden skewers with your favorite vegetables in between the chicken chunks. If using wooden skewers, soak in water for 10 to 15 minutes. You don't want them catching fire when grilling.

Vegetable Options

red, green, or yellow bell peppers   onions (red or yellow)
zucchini   parboiled small new red potatoes

When using skewers, use double skewers to keep food from twirling. It works much better. Threading double skewers is easy. Use one hand to hold two skewers, about 1/2 inch apart upright on a table, then thread the chicken and vegetables on both skewers at once.

Mixed Rice with Pecans and Raisins

Serves 6-8.

1/2 cup wild rice   1/3 cup olive oil
1 cup Basmati, Jasmine, or your favorite rice   1/2 cup orange juice
7 1/2 cups chicken stock or water   2 t salt
1 1/4 cup raisins, yellow or black   black pepper to taste
grated rind of 1 large orange   1 1/4 cup toasted pecans
5 scallions (green onions), thinly sliced   1/4 cup chopped fresh mint

Can be made ahead and frozen in a ZLB. Add toasted pecans and fresh mint when getting ready to serve. Rinse rice with cold water in a strainer. Place rice in medium-size sauce pan and add stock or water. Bring to a rapid boil. Adjust heat to a simmer and cook uncovered for about 30-45 minutes. Rice should not be too soft. Place a thin towel inside a colander and drain rice. Transfer rice to a bowl and add rest of ingredients and gently toss. Let stand an hour to allow flavors to develop. Serve and enjoy. When making ahead of time, just heat up and add pecans and mint.

Yummy Brownies

Serves 12.

6 T cocoa   1/2 t Mexican vanilla
6 T butter   1 cup chopped roasted walnuts or pecans
1 cup sugar   1/4 cup flour
2 eggs   1/4 t salt

Melt cocoa and butter over very low heat in a heavy saucepan. Remove from the heat and stir in sugar. Beat in eggs and vanilla. Stir in walnuts, flour, and salt. Spread the batter in a well-greased 10-inch DO. Bake 25 to 35 minutes at 325°. Let cool 5 to 10 minutes before slicing.

Before Trip:

- Make Horsey D's, put in ZLB and freeze.
- Make marinade for chicken, put in MSB with chicken and freeze.
- Make rice, put in ZLB and freeze.
- Toast pecans, put in ZLB and freeze.
- Mix dry ingredients for brownies, put in ZLB.
- Put wet ingredients in plastic containers.

On Trip:

- Get coals ready for grilling and making brownies.
- Start soaking skewers if wooden.
- Set out nuts and seeds.
- Place chicken and vegetables on skewers.
- Heat rice dish.
- Mix up brownies and put in DO and bake.

Menu One
Days 13-18

Breakfast

Hot Oatmeal and Cream of Wheat with Toppings

Toasted Bagels with Preserves/Jams and Spice Butter

Turkey Bacon

Lunch

Pimento Cheese Sandwiches with Coleslaw

Kosher Dill Pickles

Gingersnaps

Dinner

Cream Cheese with Black Cherry Sauce

Penne with Sweet and Sour Onion Sauce

LeSeur French Peas with Pine Nuts, Mushrooms, and Rosemary

Spiced Peaches

Sauvignon Blanc, Barbera, Sangiovese, or Viognier

This section (Days 13-18) was the most challenging of all. Fortunately, today there is a variety of good canned, dried, and packaged foods that are great for longer trips. The DO is a good way to make fabulous meals toward the end of a trip. If you have made it this far, you are now an expert at getting your ingredients together and making preparations before the trip. So in this section I have not given as much detail in the "Before Trip" instructions.

Hot Oatmeal and Cream of Wheat
with Toppings

You can buy the small individual packets of oatmeal or cream of wheat or the large containers. Toppings can be a combination of the following or used separately. Experiment.

Dried Fruits: cranberries, pears, plums, apricots, cherries, raisins, figs, peaches

Nuts: toasted pecans, toasted walnuts, toasted chopped almonds

Other: maple syrup, brown sugar, vanilla, nutmeg, cinnamon

The most perfect bowl of oatmeal is using steel-cut oats, the kind Scottish and Irish people eat. It does take 25-30 minutes to prepare but is worth it if you have a layover day or don't mind getting up a little earlier. Below is a topping I think is very good on any hot cereal.

Maple Fig Topping with Vanilla and Cinnamon
Makes 1 cup for 4 servings.

5 oz. dried figs (about 1 cup), quartered and stemmed   1/8 t vanilla
1 1/2 T maple syrup or honey   1/8 t cinnamon

Bring figs, maple, 1 1/2 T water, vanilla and cinnamon to a simmer in small saucepan over medium-high heat; cook until liquid reduces to a glaze, about 4 minutes. Spoon over oatmeal.

Spice Butter For Bagels

1/2 cup butter, slightly softened
1/4 t cinnamon or nutmeg

Mix ingredients together. Put into a plastic container in refrigerator until ready for use.

Before Trip:

- Put cereals in ZLB bag.
- Put all nuts and dried fruits in ZLB.
- Make the fig topping, put in ZLB and refrigerate up to one week before trip. Also easy to make on trip. Just put all ingredients in separate containers/ZLB.
- Make spice butter. Can be frozen for one month. Keep refrigerated on trip.

On Trip:

- Set everything out and let everyone help themselves. You can also give people a choice and make up a pot of oatmeal and a pot of cream of wheat.
- Fry bacon and toast bagels in a skillet with a little butter, or on an open fire that has good coals for toasting. Or use a toaster on your stove top if you have one.
- Set out butter and jams.

Pimento Cheese Sandwiches with Coleslaw

Makes 5-6 sandwiches.
Make the night before you eat it and keep cold. You can also add the mayonnaise right before you serve it.

1 lb each of white and yellow sharp cheddar cheese, grated
fresh ground black pepper to taste

1/2 cup to 1 cup mayonnaise
bread
dill pickles (opt.)

Coleslaw with Vinaigrette Dressing

1 small head cabbage, chopped
1 small red or yellow onion, chopped (opt.)

1 large carrot, peeled and grated
1/4 cup raisins or currants

Mix all ingredients and add vinaigrette dressing.

Vinaigrette Dressing

2 T red or white wine vinegar
pinch of dried basil
2 t Dijon mustard

8 T virgin or extra virgin olive oil
1-2 T chopped fresh herbs, such as parsley, oregano, thyme
salt and pepper to taste

Mix all ingredients in the order given. Store in refrigerator. Add to coleslaw a few hours before serving, if possible.

When putting the sandwiches together, spread the pimento cheese on the bread then pile on the coleslaw and dill pickles. I really love this combination and it is satisfying to the taste buds.

Gingersnaps

Makes 2-3 dozen small cookies.
I've had this recipe since 1964. A childhood friend of mine gave it to me in the eighth grade. Oh dear, now you know how old I am. They look and smell good, as well as taste great.

1 stick softened butter
2 cups sugar
2 eggs
1/2 cup molasses

4 cups flour
2 t baking soda
2 t cinnamon
2 t ginger

Cream butter and sugar, mix in eggs and molasses. Add dry ingredients and stir. Roll into 1-inch to 2-inch balls, then in a small bowl of sugar. Place on cookie sheet 2-3 inches apart and bake at 350° for about 15 minutes.

This is a vegetarian meal.

Cream Cheese
with Black Cherry Sauce

Makes 2 cups. Serves 8.

1 lb black cherry preserves
1/3 cup prepared mustard, Dijon is fine
dash of soy sauce (opt.)

1/8 cup Creole mustard,
1/4 cup horseradish
2 8-oz. packages of cream cheese

Puree preserves in food processor. Add remaining ingredients and blend. Keep refrigerated. Can also make several months in advance and frozen.

Serve over cream cheese with Bremner or other plain crackers, or as a dipping sauce for fried foods such as shrimp or chicken. Oh, so yummy.

Penne Pasta
with Sweet and Sour Onion Sauce

Serves 8.

2 lbs red onions
1/2 cup (1 stick) butter
3 T olive oil
3/4 t salt
1-2 cloves garlic, minced (opt.)
1 quart peeled diced canned tomatoes (with liquid)
2 cup dry red wine
1/2 t dried basil, crushed
1/2 t dried rosemary, crushed

1 large bay leaf
dash of marjoram
fresh ground pepper to taste
1 t sugar
dash of cinnamon
2 t red wine vinegar
1/4 cup dried currants
2 lbs penne pasta

Peel the onions, halve them, and slice them. Sauté them in the butter and the olive oil on medium/low heat stirring for about 1/2 hour until they are evenly light brown. Add salt and the garlic and cook another few minutes. Add all other ingredients except the pasta. Simmer on low heat for 1 1/2 to 2 hours, until it is quite thick. Cool completely before freezing in a plastic container. This can be made on your trip but requires less time if made beforehand.

On your trip just reheat the sauce and boil your pasta in several quarts of water until it is just al dente, then drain it. Toss together the pasta and sauce. You've got a great dish that took very little preparation on the river.

LeSeur French Peas

with Pine Nuts, Mushrooms, and Rosemary

Serves 8.

3 T butter
1 small yellow or white onion
10 T pine nuts, toasted at home
3 cans of LeSeur peas, drained
2 small cans sliced mushrooms, drained
1 T fresh rosemary or 1 t dried crushed rosemary
salt and pepper to taste

Sauté onion in butter, add pine nuts, continue cooking 1-2 minutes, add peas and mushrooms. Cook until heated through. Add rosemary, salt and pepper.

Spiced Peaches

Serves 8-10.

2 29-oz. cans cling peach halves or peach slices
1 cup cider vinegar
2 t whole cloves

1 1/3 cups sugar
4 cinnamon sticks
8 T brandy or rum

Drain peaches, reserving syrup. Combine the syrup in a saucepan with rest of ingredients except brandy. Bring to a boil, simmer 10 minutes. Add brandy. Pour hot syrup over peaches. Let cool. Store in refrigerator in large glass jars. Transfer to plastic container or MSB before trip. This can last several weeks in your refrigerator at home or on a trip. Just be sure you remove the cinnamon and cloves after 3-4 days or the spices will take over in a big way.

Before Trip:

- Make Black Cherry sauce and refrigerate/freeze.
- Make pasta sauce and freeze.
- Make spiced peaches.

On Trip:

- Pour Black Cherry sauce over cream cheese and set out crackers.
- Heat pasta sauce.
- Heat water for pasta.
- Make peas.
- Put spiced peaches in a nice bowl to be served.

Menu Two
Days 13-18

Breakfast

Ratatouille Omelets

Warmed Flour Tortillas

Lunch

Chicken Sandwiches with Poblano Pesto

Orange Sections

Mixed Nuts

Dinner

Cheese Board with Crackers

Vegetarian Chili

Cheddar Cornbread

Crunchy Salad

Dried Figs in Red Wine

Zinfandel

Ratatouille Omelets

For Ratatouille recipe refer to Menu 9, Days 5-12.

Allow two eggs per person and 1/2 cup Ratatouille per person.

Heat Ratatouille.

Making omelets is one of the simplest and impressive dishes you can make. Spray a skillet with oil or you can use butter. I use a 6-8-inch skillet. Mix your eggs, pour about 2 of them into a hot skillet, swirl around until the egg is almost cooked, add the heated Ratatouille in the center of the omelet. Fold one side of the egg over Ratatouille. Tilt pan to the edge of the plate and let omelet roll onto the plate. With a few practices you'll have it learned in no time. You can also add grated Monterey Jack cheese on top of the Ratatouille before folding the omelet. Serve with warm buttered tortillas. For warming tortillas refer to Menu 3, Days 1-4.

Before Trip: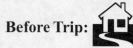

- Make Ratatouille and freeze.
- Buy tortillas and freeze.
- Don't forget the eggs, oil, and butter.

On Trip:

- Heat Ratatouille.
- Heat tortillas.
- Mix eggs.
- Make omelets.

Chicken Sandwich

with Poblano Pesto

I like this pesto because it has a slight kick to it from the poblanos. You can mix the chicken and pesto together or use the pesto as a spread, which is what I do.

> 1 6-oz. can chicken per person
> bread for sandwiches, your choice, I use thick buns and pile it on.

Poblano Pesto

Makes 1 cup.

> 4 poblano peppers, red have more heat
> 2 T minced garlic
> 1/4 cup roasted walnut pieces
> 1/4 cup cilantro or parsley
> 1/8 t lime juice
> 1/2 cup grated Parmesan cheese
> 1/4 cup extra virgin olive oil
> 4 slices smoked provolone cheese

I remove the seeds and stems before roasting because it is easier. I use rubber gloves just in case the peppers are really hot. I've burned my eyes one too many times. Ouch!

Roast the poblanos over an open flame or under a preheated oven broiler, I usually do them in my toaster oven, until the skin blisters and chars. Put peppers in a brown or plastic bag, seal and set aside about 10-15 minutes. After removing peppers from the bag and peeling off the skins, combine all other ingredients in a food processor or blender and mix. Slowly drizzle the olive oil into the food processor. This can be made a month in advance and frozen. This is enough for 4 sandwiches.

Before Trip:

- Make pesto and freeze.

On Trip:

- Make sandwiches.
- Set out oranges and nuts.

Cheese Board
with Crackers

Assortment of cheeses and crackers. Hard cheeses will last longer.

Vegetarian Chili

Serves 6 with 1 cup servings.
This recipe is so good you don't even miss the meat, and being from Texas I like meat in my chili.

1/2 lb (1 1/4 cups) red kidney, pinto, and/or black beans, washed and drained.	2 T vegetable oil
	2 T chopped parsley
1 t salt	2 T dry red wine
1 14-oz.can diced tomatoes	1 T tomato paste (can buy in a tube)
1/2 cup raw bulgur wheat	1 T fresh lemon juice
2 garlic cloves, peeled	1 1/2 T Chimayo chile powder,
1 small onion, peeled and quartered	or a combination of chile powder and cumin
1 celery rib, cut into 1-inch pieces	1/4 t Tabasco sauce, or to taste
1 medium carrot, peeled and cut into 1" pieces	fresh ground black pepper
1 small green pepper, cored and quartered	1/2 cup shredded cheddar cheese

You can use canned beans, or if using dried, soak beans with 3 cups water in a 4-quart saucepan for three hours. Drain, and add another 2 cups of water and salt, bring to boil. Reduce heat to low and cook, covered, until beans are tender, about one hour. Set aside.

Strain the liquid from the canned tomatoes into a small saucepan, reserving the tomatoes. Bring the tomato liquid to a boil, add the bulgur, cover and set aside, off the heat, for 20 minutes.

Use the metal blade of a food processor and with the machine running, drop garlic through the feed tube and process until minced. Add the onion until coarsely chopped. Set aside. Use the metal blade to process the celery, carrot, and green pepper, turning the machine on and off 6-8 times until coarsely chopped. Set aside. Then process the tomatoes until pureed, about 15 seconds.

Heat oil in large skillet over moderate heat. Add garlic and onion and cook, stirring until onion is tender, about 3 minutes. Add rest of ingredients except the cheese. Cook another 5 minutes, stirring often, or until vegetables are barely tender.

Stir vegetables and soaked bulgur into the undrained beans. Put in a double ZLB or MSB and freeze up to 2-3 months. Serve with cheddar cheese on top.

Cheddar Cornbread

Serves 5-6.

3-oz. sharp cheddar cheese (white or yellow) finely grated
1 large scallion, including green top, trimmed and finely diced, or 1/8 cup onion
1 cup white flour
1/3 cup yellow cornmeal
2 t baking powder
1/2 t baking soda
1/2 t salt
1 T sugar
3/4 cup sour cream or drained yogurt
1/3 cup vegetable oil
2 large eggs

Lightly oil a 10-inch DO. Mix all ingredients in a bowl in above order and stir just until ingredients are combined, should still have lumps. Pour batter into DO and bake for about 20 minutes at 375°. When finished baking, take lid off and cool for 5 minutes.

Crunchy Salad

Serves 5-6.

1 very small head cabbage, red or green, chopped
3/4 cup currants or raisins
1 cup toasted peanuts, shelled
1/4 cup sunflower seeds, toasted
1/4 cup poppy seeds
1/4 cup sesame seeds, toasted

Mix together and add the dressing.

Balsamic Dressing

2-3 T balsamic vinegar
1 t Dijon mustard
1 t maple syrup or brown sugar
1/4 t minced garlic
1/2 cup virgin or extra virgin olive oil

Mix all ingredients except oil. Then slowly whisk in oil. You can also put all ingredients into a jar and shake. Store in an MSB for trip. Keep refrigerated.

Dried Figs in Red Wine

Makes 2 cups, enough for 4-6 depending on serving size.
This is easy and will keep for months. Dried figs vary in dryness. I try to use chewy moist figs. If your figs are really dry, rinse quickly under water before combining with wine.

1 1/2 cups red wine (whatever style you like)
2 bay leaves
wide, 1-inch strip of orange zest, removed with a vegetable peeler
8-oz. dried Black Mission figs (about 20 large or 36 small figs)
about 1 t honey

Place wine in a small saucepan with bay leaves and simmer to 1/2 cup. While wine is reducing, cut figs in half and place in a ZLB or MSB that holds 2 to 4 cups of storage space. Put orange zest in with figs. Add honey to reduced wine, stir, pour over figs. Tightly seal bag and shake. Leave out for a few days, shaking a few times to redistribute the scant wine syrup, then refrigerate. Serve at outdoor temperature.

Before Trip:

- Make chili.
- Get ingredients together for cheddar cornbread.
- Get ingredients together for salad.
- Make dressing for salad.
- Make dried figs in wine.

On Trip:

- Set out crackers and cheeses.
- Get coals ready for DO.
- Heat chili.
- Mix up cheddar cornbread and start baking in DO.
- Make salad.
- Set out fig dessert.

Menu Three

Days 13-18

Breakfast

Bean and Cheese Burritos

Salsa Bar

Lunch

Spiced Cream Cheese Bagel Sandwiches

Copper Carrots

Dinner

Cup of Soup

Chicken Cacciatore

Salad of Artichokes, Olives, and Feta

Baked Italian Bread

Cherries in Brandy with Gingered Shortbread

Sangiovese, Barbera

Bean and Cheese Burritos

Allow 3/4 cup of beans, 1/2 cup cheese, and 2 to 3 tortillas per person.

For preparing refried beans and warming tortillas refer to Menu 3, Days 1-4.

Let everyone assemble their own burrito.

Grab a hot tortilla. Put it on your plate and add the cheese (Asadero, sharp cheddars, or Monterey Jack are good), beans, and salsa. Roll up tightly and gorge yourself and hopefully you will come back for seconds.

Before Trip: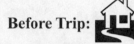

- Make beans and freeze.
- Buy 2 to 3 different kinds of salsas or make your own and freeze ahead.
- Buy tortillas and freeze.

On Trip:

- Heat beans.
- Prepare cheese.
- Set out salsas.
- Heat tortillas.
- Assemble burritos.

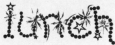

Spiced Cream Cheese Bagel Sandwiches

Makes 6 sandwiches.

1 6-oz package cream cheese, softened	2 t fresh grated orange peel (opt.)
1/2 t pumpkin pie spice	4 T chopped nuts, I like roasted pecans or walnuts
1 cup grated sharp cheddar cheese	6 bagels, sliced in half

In a bowl, combine all ingredients, except bagels and nuts, if made in advance. Add nuts just before spreading on a bagel.

Copper Carrots

Serves 12.
This is always a good old standby and can be made on the trip with fresh or canned carrots. It also keeps up to two weeks in an MSB refrigerated. If you have never experienced this recipe you really should try it. It is easy and surprisingly good.

1 lb fresh carrots, peeled, sliced in 1/4 to 1/2-inch rounds,
cooked, but still crispy, or 3 16-oz. cans sliced carrots, drained
1 very small purple onion, chopped
1 bell pepper, chopped (opt.)
1 10 1/2-oz. can condensed tomato soup
1/2 cup vegetable or olive oil
3/4 cup cider or red wine vinegar
1 cup sugar, or 1/2 cup maple syrup
1 t Dijon mustard
1 t Worcestershire sauce
1 t salt
1 t pepper

Combine all ingredients in MSB or ZLB and let marinate for 2-3 days. Drain and serve cold or at outdoor temperature. This is a rare recipe in which a canned vegetable can be used as successfully as its fresh counterpart.

Before Trip:

- Buy all ingredients for sandwiches. Can be made up to one week before consuming.
- Buy all ingredients for copper carrots. Make ahead or on trip.

On Trip:

- Set out sandwich ingredients and sliced bagels.
- Set out copper carrots.
- Set out candy bars of your choice.

Chicken Cacciatore

Serves 6.

3 10-oz. cans chicken breasts	1 1/2 t salt
4 T olive oil or butter	1/4 t pepper
1 large onion, sliced	1/2 t oregano
1 9-oz. can of mushrooms, sliced,	1/2 t marjoram
or small whole mushrooms in jars, drained	1/2 t thyme
2 small cloves of garlic, minced	1/2 cup dry white wine
2 14.5-oz. cans chopped tomatoes, can use plain	Parmesan cheese
diced tomatoes, or Italian hcrb, mushroom, or garlic	wild rice
2 chicken bouillon cubes	capers (opt.)

Prepare wild rice according to package instructions. Open cans of chicken, drain liquid, set aside. Sauté, onion, garlic, and mushrooms. Stir in tomatoes, bouillon cubes, seasonings, and white wine. Cook a few minutes. Add chicken and simmer 5 minutes. Serve on or beside rice and sprinkle with Parmesan.

Salad of Artichokes, Olives, and Feta

Serves 6-8.

4 14-oz. cans artichokes	1 14-oz. can olives
1/4-1/2 lb Feta cheese	1 bottle of Italian salad dressing or make your own below

Italian Dressing

Makes 1/2 cup.

1/4 cup olive oil	2 T lemon juice
1 t lemon zest,	1/4 t salt
1/2 t thyme	1 clove garlic, pressed or minced
1 T fresh grated Romano cheese	1/2 t ground pepper

Mix all ingredients well. Chill and serve. Store in MSB for trip. Will last several weeks refrigerated.

Italian Bread

Buy 1-2 cans (the cylinder shaped rolls/bread that you pop open) in refrigerator section of grocery store. Refer to Menu 4, Days 1-4 on preparation of rolls/bread.

Cherries in Brandy

Serves 4-5.

6-oz. red currant or black cherry jelly
1/4 cup brandy or cognac

1 lb fresh or frozen pitted sweet cherries

Melt jelly in a saucepan and add cherries. Cook for 5 minutes. Let cool. Add brandy and chill one hour. Transfer to an MSB and freeze before your trip. Will last 2 to 3 months in your freezer. If you need to store it in a cooler without ice this can be done up to 5 to 6 days.

Gingered Shortbread

You can make these in advance and store outside of a cooler. They have a great ginger taste.
Serves 8-10.

1 cup (2 sticks) unsalted butter, cold
1/2 cup sugar
1 3/4 cup flour, sifted

1 cup rice flour (if unavailable, mix together
1/2 cup cornstarch and 1/2 cup white flour)
1/2 t kosher salt or regular salt
1 T ground ginger, sometimes I use fresh, very finely minced

Mix the sugar into the butter with a pastry blender until well mixed. Combine dry ingredients and mix into the butter and sugar until well blended. I use my hands and a mixer, or even a food processor is fine. Shape dough into a ball, it will be crumbly. Wrap and chill in refrigerator 10 minutes. Preheat oven to 350°. Pat dough into a well buttered 8-inch pie pan. Cut lightly into the dough to mark off 8-10 portions. Cool in pan. Can be frozen for two months. They are fragile so keep them in a spot where they won't become just crumbs. Unless you want crumbs to sprinkle over your cherries. Hey, that might be good!

Before Trip:

- Buy cups of soup, maybe Italian.
- Get chicken, rice, and salad ingredients together.
- Make or buy dressing.
- Make cherries and cookies.

On Trip:

- Boil water for cups of soup.
- Prepare DO coals for bread.
- Prepare wild rice.
- Prepare Chicken Cacciatore.
- Bake bread in DO.
- Prepare salad.
- Set out dessert and you are done.

Menu Four

Days 13-18

Breakfast

Smoked Trout Hash with Spicy Catsup

Scrambled Eggs

Lunch

Couscous Salad

Dried Fruit Mixture

Assortment of Hard Candies

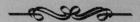

Dinner

Canned Tostitos/Torengo Chips with Two Salsas

Amigo Pie

Slaw with Marinated Artichokes

Mexican Cookies

Gewurztraminer/Chenin Blanc

Smoked Trout Hash
with Spicy Catsup

Serves 8.

Spicy Catsup

3/4 cup catsup   1 T maple syrup
1 t Tabasco sauce   1 T cider vinegar

Trout Hash

8 cups 1/4-inch cubes Idaho potatoes   salt and pepper to taste
3 T olive oil   12 oz. smoked rainbow trout, flaked,
1 1/2 cups chopped onions   or other smoked fish (can use canned fish)
3 garlic cloves, minced   2 T parsley
2 t rosemary

Combine first 4 ingredients in a bowl and mix. You can make this ahead of time and store in an MSB in the refrigerator. It will keep several weeks.

Blanch potatoes in boiling water in a saucepan for two minutes. Drain and pat dry. Sauté potatoes in oil in skillet until crisp. Add onions, cook 1 minute. Stir in garlic, rosemary, salt and pepper. Stir in trout and parsley. Cook until heated. Keep warm while you make the scrambled eggs.

Scrambled Eggs

Serves 8.

1 dozen eggs, can use the kind that come in cartons, or powdered
4 T olive oil or butter
salt and pepper to taste

Heat skillet with olive oil, when hot add mixed eggs to the skillet and stir until you have them cooked to your liking. Everyone can't believe the way I like mine cooked, like rubber; you can throw against a wall and they bounce off. Divide hash and eggs up and drizzle catsup mixture all over in a zigzag pattern.

Before Trip:

- Buy all ingredients.
- Make spicy catsup.

On Trip:

- Make hash and scrambled eggs.

Couscous Salad

2 cup cooked couscous
1 cup canned carrots
1/2 cup chopped, roasted red bell pepper, can used canned peppers or in a jar
1/4 cup olive oil
1 T malt or cider vinegar
1 T tamari or soy sauce
1 t Dijon mustard
1 t garlic granules
2 T water
2 T parsley
1/2 t dill
1/2 t marjoram
2 T capers in balsamic vinegar

You can also add canned shrimp, tuna, turkey, or chicken to this recipe.

Cook couscous according to package and toss with carrots and bell pepper. Blend rest of ingredients in a jar and shake. Pour over couscous and enjoy.

Before Trip:

- Buy ingredients for couscous, dried mixed fruit, and candies.

On Trip:

- Make couscous after breakfast to be eaten at lunch, or the day before you serve it.
- Set out fruit and candies.

Amigo Pie

Serves 14.
This is always a big hit with people and doesn't require much time. We made it the last night on the
Grand Canyon and it was spectacular.

Filling

1 cup coarsely chopped sun-dried tomatoes or 2 cups diced canned tomatoes

2 1/2 cups chopped onion (1 very large yellow onion), or use dried minced onion

3 T olive oil

4 15-oz. cans Stag brand chili (no beans), or your favorite brand

15-oz. can corn

5 T ground Chimayo chile or 7 T regular chili powder

1 1/2 15-oz. cans small pitted ripe olives

Crust

2 1/2 cups corn meal

3/4 cup flour

3/4 t salt

1 T baking powder

3 1/4 cups hot water

6 T margarine or butter (melted in the water) or olive oil

1 1/2 15-oz. cans pitted ripe olives, sliced

5 cup shredded cheddar or parmesan cheese

1 can Torengo chips (tortilla chips in a can)

Boil sun-dried tomatoes in water to cover. Sauté onion in olive oil. Add chili, tomatoes, corn, ground chile, and olives and heat through. Combine corn meal, flour, salt, and baking powder. Add water and margarine and mix until smooth. Stir in half of the cheese and the olives. Pour cornmeal mixture into greased DOs (one 12-inch and one 10-inch). Spoon the meat mixture into center of cornmeal mixture. Lightly press down. Bake in hot DO at 400° for 25 minutes or until pie is bubbling. Top with the remaining cheese and ancho chile or other red sauce, if desired. Just before serving stand up the Torengo chips on top in an artistic pattern for a nice effect. You'll wow everyone.

Topping: Ancho Chile Red Sauce (opt.) (makes about 2 cups)

10 to 12 dried whole ancho chiles

3 cloves garlic, chopped

1 large onion, chopped

3 cups water

Place chiles on baking pan in a 250° oven for about 15 minutes until chiles smell like they are toasted, but don't let burn. Remove stems and seeds and crumble into sauce pan. Add remaining ingredients, bring to a boil, reduce heat and simmer for 20 to 30 minutes until chiles are soft. Puree the mixture, then strain through a sieve. I usually cook it down a little more if I want a thicker sauce. This is a nice rich sauce for just about anything Mexican and you can substitute different peppers. Freeze in MSB. It will keep in the cooler even after the ice is gone.

Amigo Pie, Page 190

Slaw with Marinated Artichokes, Page 191

Slaw with Marinated Artichokes

Serves 8.

1 small head of cabbage, chopped
4 small jars marinated artichokes
1 14.5-oz. can garbanzo beans
salt and pepper to taste
bottled Italian dressing of your choice

Add all ingredients together, mix, and serve.

Mexican Cookies

Makes 3 dozen.
These cookies are easy to make and delicious. A nice way to end a Mexican dinner.

1 cup butter (not margarine)
3/4 cup powdered sugar
2 cups flour
1 t vanilla
1 cup finely chopped pecans
1/2 cup plain or colored sugar (my favorite and pretty), or 1 1/2 cups powdered sugar.

These are best made ahead of time. The colored sugar holds up better if you are having this late in your trip. In a large bowl, beat butter until fluffy. Add next three ingredients. Mix well. Blend in pecans. Shape into 1-inch balls and roll in colored sugar and place 1 inch apart on baking sheet. Bake at 325° until pale golden brown, about 20 to 25 minutes. Cool on wire rack. Powdered sugar option: when slightly cool, roll in powdered sugar, then finish cooling. Put in plastic container and freeze until trip.

Before Trip:

- Make cookies and store in freezer.
- Buy ingredients for entire dinner.
- Make Ancho Chile sauce and freeze in MSB.

On Trip:

- Set out chips and salsas.
- Heat coals for Amigo Pie.
- Mix up Amigo Pie and put in DO to bake.
- Make salad.
- Set out cookies.

Mexican Cookies, Page 191

Menu Five
Days 13-18

Breakfast

Peanut or Almond Butter Granola

Fruit Bars

Lunch

Chinese Chicken Salad

Chinese Crackers

Dried Apples

Selection of Pepperidge Farm Cookies

Dinner

Gourmet Breadsticks/Crackers with Mustard Dipping Sauce

Salmon Casserole

Medley of Creamed Vegetables

Cherry Maple Syrup Sauce over Shortcake

Chardonnay

Peanut or Almond Butter Granola

Serves 8-10.

> 1 cup raisins
> 1/2 cup dried Black Mission figs, snipped and quartered
> 2/3 cup creamy peanut or almond butter
> 2/3 cup honey
> 1/2 teaspoon cinnamon
> 1 teaspoon vanilla extract
> 4 cups oatmeal
> 1 cup shelled peanuts or slivered almonds

Pour boiling water over raisins and figs to cover; let stand 10 minutes; drain. In saucepan, combine peanut butter, honey and cinnamon; heat through. Remove from heat; stir in vanilla extract. Place oats in large shallow roasting pan or 15 x 10 x 1-inch baking pan. Pour warm peanut butter mixture over oats and stir gently until all the mixture is coated; spread evenly in pan. Bake at 300 degrees F for 35 to 40 minutes, stirring occasionally. Turn off oven; stir in raisins, figs and nuts. Let dry in oven 1 1/2 hours, stirring occasionally.

Before Trip: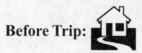

- Make granola.
- Buy fruit/breakfast bars (1 to 2 per person).

On Trip:

- Set out granola and fruit bars.

Chinese Chicken Salad

Serves 5-6.
It's truly tasty and satisfying.

> 4 10-oz. cans chicken breasts
> 1/4 cup chopped onion
> 1/2 cup slivered almonds, toasted
> 1/4 cup sesame seeds, toasted
> 1/4 cup peanuts, roasted (opt.)

Combine above ingredients.

Dressing

> 4 T sugar
> 1 t salt
> 1 t Dijon mustard
> 4 T red wine vinegar
> 4 T soy sauce
> 3 slices fresh ginger peeled
> 2 cloves of garlic, slightly mashed
> 1/2 cup olive oil

Combine above ingredients in a jar and shake well. Refrigerate overnight to blend flavors. Remove ginger and garlic from dressing so it isn't too strong. You can store this in an MSB.

Before Trip:

- Make dressing and put in MSB in refrigerator.
- Roast nuts and put in ZLB in refrigerator.

On Trip:

- Make chicken salad with dressing.
- Set out crackers, dried apples, and cookies.

Mustard Dipping Sauce

Makes about 1 cup.

1/2 cup Dijon mustard
1/2 cup good olive oil
1 envelope Good Seasons Italian salad dressing mix

3 T light brown sugar or maple syrup
1 T cider or wine vinegar

Combine all ingredients, stirring until smooth. Serve with gourmet breadsticks or crackers. This is also good with vegetables, shrimp, or grilled chicken kabobs. It is nice chilled if possible.

Salmon Casserole

Serves 6-8.

4 eggs, powdered is fine
3 6-oz. cans of salmon, drained and flaked
1/4 t black pepper

23.5-oz. can creamed corn
2 t instant minced onion (or 1 small onion finely diced)
1/2 to 3/4 cup garlic bread crumbs, cheddar cheese, or both

Make this in a lightly oiled 10-inch DO. In a medium bowl, beat eggs, add remaining ingredients except crumbs and mix well. Pour into the DO, sprinkle with crumbs, cheese, or both. Bake at 350° for 30-45 minutes or until firm.

Medley of Creamed Vegetables

Serves 6-8.
My Mom used to make creamed peas for us as part of our Sunday dinner with a roast and potatoes. I loved the creamed peas.

You can use any combination of vegetables.

1 15-oz. can peas, drained
1 15-oz. can carrots, drained

1 15-oz. can corn, drained

White Sauce
Makes 1 cup.

2 T butter or margarine
2 T white flour
1/4 t salt

1 cup milk, fresh, canned, or powdered
dash of pepper

Melt butter in sauce pan over low heat. Blend in flour, salt, and pepper. Add milk, whisk constantly until mixture thickens and bubbles. Add drained vegetables and heat.

Rio Grande, TX   (James Machin)

Cherry Maple Syrup Sauce over Shortcake Page, 197

Shortcake

Serves 8.

2 cups flour
2 T sugar
3 t baking powder
1/2 t salt

1/2 cup butter or margarine
1 beaten egg (powdered in fine)
2/3 cup milk (can use powdered) or light cream

Sift together dry ingredients. Cut in butter until mixture resembles coarse crumbs. Combine egg and milk, add, stirring just to moisten. Spread dough in greased 10-inch DO, building up edges slightly. Bake 450° for 10-15 minutes. Cool 5 minutes. Cut 8 pieces. Remove from pan. Split in two layers, lift off tops and fill with cherries (see below), put tops back on and ladle some cherries on top. Yummy! For fun you could also make a chocolate shortcake, just grate in your favorite chocolate.

Cherry Maple Syrup Sauce

Makes about 2 cups.
This recipe can be made in advance and put in MSB and refrigerated. It can also be made on the trip.

2 cups pitted dark sweet cherries,
I use cherries in jars or cans, drained
1/2 cup maple syrup
1/3 cup fresh orange juice
1 t lemon zest

1 T cornstarch
3 T cognac
2 T unsalted butter, cut into bits
lemon juice to taste

In a saucepan combine the first four ingredients. Bring liquid to a simmer, stirring occasionally, for 5 minutes. In a small bowl dissolve the cornstarch in 2 T of cognac. Bring cherry mixture to a boil and stir in cornstarch mixture and cook over low heat, stirring until thickened. Remove pan from heat. Stir in butter and lemon juice. Let sauce cool at room temperature. Add 1 T of remaining cognac, cover until ready to serve. Will last 3 weeks in refrigerator. This is also delicious served warm over ice cream, chocolate pound cake, or sponge cake.

Before Trip:

- Make mustard dipping sauce and put in an MSB in refrigerator.
- Get ingredients together for dinner.
- Make cherry maple syrup sauce.

On Trip: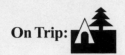

- Set out mustard dipping sauce, breadsticks/crackers.
- Start coals for salmon and shortcake.
- Make salmon casserole and start baking.
- Mix up shortcake and put in DO ready to bake.
- Make vegetables.
- Warm cherry maple sauce.
- Bake shortbread while eating dinner, or you can stack this DO on top of the salmon.

Menu Six
Days 13-18

Breakfast

Buttermilk and Toasted Nut Pancakes

Cinnamon Applesauce

Lunch

Rice Salad with Orange, Olives, and Almonds

Wheat Crackers

Selection of Granola Bars

Dinner

Pot of Soup

Chicken Noodle Dish

Cranberry Sauce

Maple Sweet Potato Casserole

Port with Cholcolate

Chardonnay or Riesling

Buttermilk and Roasted Nut Pancakes

Serves 6-8. Makes about 24 5-inch pancakes.
Nothing quite like buttermilk pancakes. I've found the powdered buttermilk much more to my liking.

2 cups sifted flour
1/4 t salt
2 t baking powder
1/2 t baking soda
1/8 t nutmeg
1 T sugar
2 eggs, powdered
2 cups buttermilk, powdered, usually found in baking section of grocery store
2 T melted butter or vegetable oil
1/4 t vanilla
3/4 cups roasted pecans
12 oz. pure maple syrup

Sift together all the dry ingredients. Add the appropriate amount of water for each of the powdered ingredients according to the instructions on the packages. Add more water by the tablespoon if pancakes are too thick. Add roasted pecans. Batter should be lumpy. Serve with syrup.

Cinnamon Applesauce

Serves 6.

2 14.5-oz. cans applesauce
1/2 t cinnamon

Mix together. If not sweet enough add a little maple syrup. Warm on stove top and serve with your pancakes.

Before Trip:

- Toast pecans.

On Trip:

- Make pancakes and applesauce.

Rice Salad

with Oranges, Olives, and Almonds

Serves 5-6.

2 T olive oil
1 small clove garlic, minced
1/4 t zest plus 1 T juice from 1 small orange
2 t sherry vinegar
1 t salt
1/2 t black pepper
1 recipe (see below) for cooked rice
1/3 cup coarsely chopped pitted green olives
2 medium oranges, peeled and cut into segments
1/3 cup slivered almonds, toasted
1 T oregano

Stir together oil, garlic, orange zest, juice, vinegar, salt, and pepper in a small bowl. Combine rest of ingredients and drizzle oil mixture over all and mix to combine. Nice to let stand 20 minutes for flavors to blend, if possible.

Cooked Rice

1 1/2 cups long grain or basmati rice
1 1/2 t salt

Boil 4 quarts of water. Meanwhile, heat skillet until hot, add rice and toast, stirring frequently, about 5 minutes. Add salt to water and stir in toasted rice. Return to boil and cook uncovered, until rice is tender, but not soft, 8 to10 minutes for long grain rice or about 15 minutes for basmati. Drain rice with fine-mesh strainer. Cool and add to salad ingredients.

Before Trip:

- Toast almonds.

On Trip:

- Make rice salad.
- Set out crackers and bars.

Pot of Soup

Buy a good dried soup that makes a large pot so that everyone can have a cup. Follow instructions on the package.

Chicken Noodle Dish

Serves 10-12.

8 oz. medium noodles, cooked
2 cups canned chicken breasts or turkey
1 can cream of mushroom soup, undiluted
1 can cream of chicken soup, undiluted
1 cup mayonnaise or yogurt
1 can sliced water chestnuts (opt.)

1 can sliced mushrooms, drained
1 small jar pimiento, drained and chopped
1 cup toasted slivered almonds
1 10-oz. can corn or other vegetable
8 oz. cheddar cheese, shredded,
or canned Parmesan cheese

Mix first 8 ingredients and 1/2 cup almonds in a large bowl. Place 1/2 of ingredients into 12-inch DO. Spread canned corn on top, then 1/2 of cheese. Top with remaining chicken mixture, then cheese and spread with remaining slivered almonds. Bake at 350° for 35-45 minutes. Serve with cranberry sauce.

Maple Sweet Potato Casserole

Serves 8-12.
This is one of my favorite ways to prepare sweet potatoes.

3 lbs (about 6 medium) sweet potatoes, peeled, halved
lengthwise, and halves cut crosswise into 1/4-inch slices
6 T unsalted butter, melted
5 T maple syrup

1 T grated fresh ginger or 1 t powdered
3/4 t salt
1/4 t chili powder
1/2 T cornstarch

Parboil sweet potato slices over high heat in boiling water until a paring knife easily pierces but does not break apart, 4-5 minutes. Drain potatoes well and turn into a buttered 12-inch DO. Stir melted butter, maple syrup, ginger, salt, and chile powder in a small bowl; set aside. Mix cornstarch with 2 T cold water in small bowl until totally smooth, stir into butter mixture, pour over sweet potatoes, and toss to coat well. Bake at 375° for about 40 minutes or until liquid thickens to glaze potatoes. You may want to stir it once but be careful not to break up potatoes. Don't forget to store the potatoes in a dark, dry, well-ventilated spot, out of plastic bags.

Before Trip:

- Don't forget the pot of soup. Toast almonds.
- Buy canned cranberry sauce.
- Buy and package ingredients for the sweet potato casserole.
- Buy the best chocolate and good port you can find if you want rave reviews.

On Trip:

- Start coals for two DOs. Boil water for pot of soup and serve.
- Make maple sweet potato casserole and start baking.
- Make chicken noodle dish and start baking. Put out cranberry sauce.
- Set out port and chocolate.

Menu Seven

Days 13-18

Breakfast

Scambled Eggs

Bacon

Mixed Dried Fruit

Lunch

Peanut or Almond Butter Sandwiches

Canned Chips

Assortment of Candies and Cookies

Dinner

Assorted Pretzels

Seafood and Artichoke Casserole

Baked Onions

Golden Pineapple and Caramel Cake

Chardonnay or Sauvignon Blanc

Scrambled eggs
with Salsa

Serves 4 to 6.

> 3 T butter or olive oil
> 1 small onion, diced
> 1 dozen eggs, fresh or powdered, beaten together in a bowl
> 1 small can sliced mushrooms, drained
> salt and pepper to taste
> 1 container of salsa

Melt butter or oil in skillet. Add onion and sauté for 2-3 minutes. Add eggs and mushrooms. Stir until eggs are scrambled the way you like them. Add salt and pepper. Serve the salsa on the side or on top of eggs.

Before Trip: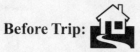

- Buy packaged, fully cooked bacon, canned bacon, or other canned meat.

On Trip:

- Make eggs and bacon.
- Set out fruit.

Peanut or Almond Butter Sandwiches

peanut butter, or I prefer almond butter
dates, figs, and/or raisins, diced and mixed
orange marmalade
bread or crackers

Use 1 T of peanut/almond butter to every 1/2 T of diced dates, figs, or raisins. Add as much marmalade as you like, and mix all together. My favorite is dates with a good English marmalade. If you don't like marmalade use any preserve, jam, or jelly. Spread on bread or crackers. This recipe can be made before your trip. It will keep about three weeks.

Before Trip:

- Make peanut butter fruit/marmalade mixture, if desired.

On Trip:

- Make sandwiches.
- Set out chips.
- Set out dessert.

CAMP BATH

BAIL BUCKET

Seafood and Artichoke Casserole

Serves 6.

> 1 small can of mushrooms
> 6 T butter
> 1 1/2 lbs canned shrimp or crab meat
> 1 15-oz. can artichoke hearts, coarsely chopped
> 1/4 cup flour
> 1 1/2 cups milk (powdered), can also use light cream
> 1/2 cup dry sherry (I use Marsala)
> 1 T Worcestershire sauce
> salt and pepper to taste
> 1/4 t paprika
> 1/2 cup Parmesan cheese

Sauté mushrooms in 2 T butter for 1 minute. Layer mushrooms, seafood, and artichoke hearts in a 10-inch DO. Melt remaining butter until foaming, add flour, cook and stir for 2-3 minutes. Stirring, gradually add milk and cook until the sauce is blended and thickened. Add sherry, Worcestershire sauce, salt, pepper, and paprika. Pour over casserole in DO and sprinkle with Parmesan. Bake at 350° 25-30 minutes until bubbly hot and lightly browned.

Baked Onions

Serves 6.

> 6 small sweet yellow onions (Texas 1015s or similar), peeled, cut in half
> 6 T brown sugar or honey
> 6 T butter
> foil

On the cut side of every 1/2 onion, cover each with 1/2 T maple syrup and 1/2 T of butter. Put cut edge of onions back together to form a whole onion and wrap each one in foil and bake over a rack of hot coals turning once or twice for about 30 minutes. You can also bake these in a DO, cut side up, with a little water in the bottom.

Golden Pineapple and Caramel Cake

Serves 8.

Topping:

1 T vegetable/canola oil
6 T (3/4 stick) unsalted butter/squeeze margarine
1 cup (packed) dark brown sugar
2 14-oz. cans chunk pineapple, drained
30 whole hazelnuts, toasted

Cake:

1 1/2 cups cake flour or self-rising flour
1 T ground almonds
1/2 t baking powder
3 large eggs, powdered
1 T amaretto
3/4 cup (1 1/2 sticks) unsalted butter, squeeze margarine
3/4 cup sugar

For Topping:

Grease bottom and sides of a 10-inch DO with the vegetable oil Melt butter in DO, add brown sugar and stir until well blended, about 1 minute. Remove from heat and arrange pineapple chunks on top of brown sugar and mound sides if possible. Place hazelnuts between pineapple spaces, create a design with them.

For Cake:

Mix first four ingredients (which already should be mixed in ZLB). Mix water for eggs and add amaretto. Cream together butter and sugar in bowl. Mix in dry ingredients alternately with amaretto mixture to the creamed butter and sugar. Spoon batter on top of pineapple. Bake at 350° for about 35-40 minutes. Put 1-2 extra coals on the bottom to caramelize the brown sugar. Cool cake in pan about 5 minutes. Run small knife around edges of pan to loosen cake and place platter over cake and invert onto platter. Serve warm. I've even served rum-spiked whipped cream with this dessert. One cup whipped cream with 2 T rum. Yummy!

Before Trip:

- Get ingredients together for dinner.
- Mix ingredients in ZLB for cake.

On Trip:

- Set out pretzels of different sizes and shapes.
- Start coals for casserole, onions, and DO dessert.
- Mix up casserole and start baking, along with onions.
- Make dessert and bake.

Menu Eight
Days 13-18

Breakfast
Maple Rice with Dried Fruits

Cashew Orange Biscotti

Lunch
Mediterranean Antipasto

Pita Chips

Mixed Nuts

Dinner
Baked Ham

Boston Brown Bread

Mixed Veggies

Two Orgasmic Chocolate Cake with Cabernet Sauvignon Sauce

Pinot Gris or Pinot Noir

Maple Rice with Dried Fruits

Any rice will do. Follow package instructions for cooking rice and add maple syrup and dried fruits to your rice with milk.

Cashew Orange Biscotti

These biscotti are equally delicious made with roasted almonds, pecans, or hazelnuts in place of the cashews. Great with coffee of course.

> 1 1/2 cups roasted cashews
> 2 cups flour
> 1 cup sugar
> 1 t baking soda
> 1/4 t salt
> 4 large eggs
> 1 T freshly grated orange zest
> 1 t vanilla
> 1 t water

Preheat oven to 300° F. Butter a large baking sheet. Coarsely chop cashews. Sift the next four ingredients into a bowl. In another bowl with an electric mixer beat together three eggs, zest, and vanilla. Stir in flour mixture and beat until a stiff dough is formed. Stir in cashews.

In small bowl beat together water and remaining egg to make an egg wash. On baking sheet with floured hands form dough into 12-inch-long logs and flatten slightly. Brush logs with the egg wash. Bake logs in middle of oven until golden, about 50 minutes. Cool logs on baking sheet on a rack for 10 minutes. On a cutting board with a serrated knife, diagonally cut logs into 1/3-inch thick slices. Arrange biscotti, cut side down, on baking sheet and bake in middle of oven until crisp, about 15 minutes. Cool on rack. Keep in airtight container up to three weeks or in freezer for 3 to 4 months.

Before Trip:

- Make biscotti.

On Trip:

- Make rice.
- Set out biscotti, don't forget to dip it in your coffee or other hot beverage.

Mediterranean Antipasto

Makes 16 to 18 cups.

1/4 cup olive oil
3-4 cloves garlic, peeled and chopped
2 T dried parsley
1 quart jar giardiniera (marinated vegetables, drained)
1 small jar pearl onions, drained
1 small jar stuffed olives, drained
2 small jars artichoke hearts, marinated
1 can pitted black olives
2 1/2 cups Greek olives
8-oz. can tomato sauce (more if preferred)
salt and pepper to taste
white vinegar to taste (opt.)
3 6-oz. cans tuna packed in olive oil

In a large pan, sauté the garlic in the olive oil, add everything above except the tuna. Add salt and pepper and a touch of vinegar to taste, stir all. Fold in tuna and mix. Can be made a few days in advance and stored in a glass jar, plastic container, or ZLB. This will last refrigerated for as long as a month.

Before Trip:

- Mix up antipasto in advance if desired. Best made on trip if you are having it later.

On Trip:

- Make antipasto.
- Set out pita chips and mixed nuts.

This was one of my first menus on a raft trip, so it is fitting that this be my last menu.
Everyone loved it. I hope you will also.

Baked Ham

Buy a canned ham, enough for everyone to have two large pieces.
Drizzle maple syrup or honey, and mustard over your ham and put it in a DO with 1/4 cup water and bake until heated through, 30-40 minutes.

Boston Brown Bread

This comes in a can in the grocery store. I usually buy two cans for 8-10 people. Partially open one end with a can opener, set on coals, and follow cooking time on can. I've also taken the bread out of the can and wrapped it in foil to warm on a grate above coals. This bread is really good. You can eat it plain as I do or butter it after it is sliced.

Two Orgasmic Chocolate Cake

with Cabernet Sauvignon Sauce

Serves 10.
The name says it all.

> 2 squares unsweetened chocolate (2 oz.), or 6 T cocoa powder
> 1 stick butter, can use squeeze margarine
> Melt these over low heat together.
> 1 cup milk (powdered), pour into butter/chocolate mixture.

Sift together:

> 1 cup flour
> 1 t soda
> 1/4 t salt

In a bowl beat together:

> 1 cup sugar
> 1 egg, powdered
> 1 t vanilla

Alternately add chocolate and dry ingredients to this in 3 portions. Makes a very thin batter. Bake at 350° for 35-40 minutes in a 10-inch DO. This is an outstanding cake for being so simple. Serve with 1-2 T of Cabernet Sauvignon sauce on each slice.

Cabernet Sauvignon Sauce

                1 bottle cabernet sauvignon
                1/2 cup sugar
                1 t vanilla
                1 whole cinnamon stick
                peel from 1 orange
                peel from 1 lemon
                2 whole cloves
                1 whole bay leaf

Add all ingredients in pan and simmer until 1 cup of liquid is left. It should coat the back of a spoon. Put in container. Can be made up to several days before trip and will keep several weeks.

This cake and sauce combination is fantastic. It lives up to its name. Need I say more? This is a good ending.

Before Trip:

- Make Cabernet Sauvignon sauce.
- Get ingredients together for dinner.

On Trip:

- Get coals started for ham, bread, and cake.
- Put ham in DO and bake.
- Put bread on coals to bake.
- Make cake and bake.
- Heat up vegetables. This should be canned. Sometimes fresh potatoes, onions, and carrots can last.

Dutch Oven Cooking Chart

This chart is not set in stone. It is approximate according to what I bake and my experiences with a Dutch oven. It is intended to give you guidelines on the amount of charcoal you will need for your trip.

I use hard anodized aluminum DOs. The aluminum surface is treated with a very hard protective oxide layer by electrolysis. It is light weight, essentially non-stick, and much easier to clean than regular aluminum or cast iron. I love mine.

Temp.	10 inch		12 inch		14 inch	
Deg. F	Top	Bottom	Top	Bottom	Top	Bottom
300	13	6	15	8	16	10
325	14	7	16	8	18	10
350*	**15**	**7**	**17**	**9**	**19**	**11**
375	16	7	18	10	20	12
400	17	8	19	10	22	12
425	18	8	20	11	23	13
450	19	9	22	11	24	13
500	21	10	24	12	27	15

Most commonly used. Use this if not otherwise specified

Charcoal Chimney: We like to stay away from using lighter fluid. A good way to start your coals is by using a chimney, a cylindrical device with a grate inside that holds the charcoal tightly together. Place some crumpled newspaper in the bottom part of the chimney and fill the top with coals. Light the paper, and, because air is directed up the chimney, the coals will be hot in a short time. When they are hot, carefully pour the coals into the grill. (It's a good idea to use channel-lock pliers for this chore.) Match light charcoal is another alternative and easy to use in starting your fire. When the coals are mostly covered with a light ash they are ready. It's not scientific. Refer to Grilling under Tips in the front of book.

If Stacking DOs: Use the "Bottom" number of coals on top of all DOs except the very top one. Use the "Top" number on top of the top one only. Otherwise, you will burn the bottom of the DO that is stacked on top. For example, if you have three DOs stacked 14"-12"-10" bottom to top, for 350 deg. the number of coals from bottom to top would be 11-11-9-15.

Coals placed on top of a DO should be placed around the outer edge of the lid, right against the lip, especially when you are stacking another one on top. Coals placed underneath the bottom DO should be placed under the outside edge, with one in the center.

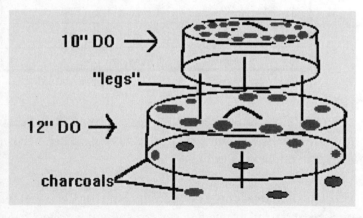

Duty Chart

This spells out everyone's responsibilities in advance. You know when you are on and when you can relax. So you don't have to feel guilty about not helping. It also spells out which coolers contain which meals. That way you only have to get into one cooler at a time, and you use it until it's empty. It saves on confusion and ice. Each cooler should be labeled as to which days it is for.

Day	Date	Kitchen Patrol	Dirt Patrol	Cooler
0	16-Aug	EdP & Libby	Duwain & Susie	EdP
1	17-Aug	EdP & Libby	Duwain & Susie	
2	18-Aug	EdP & Libby	Duwain & Susie	
3	19-Aug	Duwain & Susie	EdP & Libby	Susie
4	20-Aug	Duwain & Susie	EdP & Libby	
5	21-Aug	James & Marilynn	Gary & John	James
6	22-Aug	James & Marilynn	Gary & John	
7	23-Aug	James & Marilynn	Gary & John	
8	24-Aug	EdZ & Whart	James & Marilynn	EdZ
9	25-Aug	EdZ & Whart	James & Marilynn	
10	26-Aug	Jackie & Tom	EdZ & Whart	Tom
11	27-Aug	Jackie & Tom	EdZ & Whart	
12	28-Aug	Jackie & Tom	EdZ & Whart	
13	29-Aug	Glenn & Nancy	Jackie & Tom	Glenn
14	30-Aug	Glenn & Nancy	Jackie & Tom	
15	31-Aug	Glenn & Nancy	Jackie & Tom	Gary
16	1-Sep	Gary & John	Glenn & Nancy	
17	2-Sep	Gary & John	Glenn & Nancy	
18	3-Sep	Brewpub	Motel 6	

Kitchen Patrol duties: carry cookbox up from raft and set up, provide happy hour and/or dinner drinks, plan and prepare meals, washup cooking dishes only (each person does their individual dishes), pack up cookbox and deliver to raft next morning.

Dirt Patrol duties: carry Pooparama Unit (or PU, what we call the Groover) from rafts and set up, set up wash buckets and refill as needed, sort/crush/burn garbage, pack up garbage/PU and deliver to rafts next morning.

Day begins with dinner (cooks can set up their kitchen when you reach camp) and ends with lunch next day.

Cooking Equipment List

small DO (10")

large DO(s) (12" + 14" if needed)

channel lock pliers

charcoal chimney and charcoal

firepan

kitchen floor tarp (to catch crumbs)

coffee pot

potholders

dish towels

8- and 6-qt pots

2-qt pot

2 lids/fry pans

6-cup pot w/lid

measuring cup

bowls

dinner plates

eating utensils

plastic cups

large and medium mixing bowls

griddle

cutting board

sharp knife set

Ziploc bags

garbage bags

dishwashing sponge

pot scrubbers

dish soap

dishwater strainer

1 qt clorox

hand wash soap

hand washer (can with hole(s) in the bottom
suspended from a hanger)

paper towels

foil

table cloth

cooking oil

2 liter OJ container

can opener

pot handle

spatulas

stainless spoons

wooden spoons

grater

pasta hook

pasta strainer

tongs

soup ladle

basting brush

whisk

sugar & sweetener

creamer

coffee

tea

cocoa

toothpicks

salt & pepper

spices, hot sauce

matches & lighter

sharpie, pencil

playing cards

spare stove generator

fuel funnel

candle

Sources for Gear

Blackadar Boating
Hwy 93 North
Salmon, ID 83467
208-756-3958

Canyon R.E.O.
PO Box 3493
Flagstaff, AZ 86003
800-637-4604
http://canyonreo.com/

Cascade Outfitters
604 E. 45th Street
Boise, ID 83714
800-223-7238
http://cascadeoutfitters.com/

Cee Dub's (Dutch ovens & accessories)
HC67, Box 72
Grangeville, ID 83530
208-983-7937
http://www.ceedubs.com/

Clavey River Equipment
409 Petaluma Blvd. South
Petaluma, CA 94953-0180
800-832-4226
http://www.clavey.com/

Down River Equipment Company
12100 W. 52nd. Ave.
Wheat Ridge, CO 80033
888-467-2144
http://www.downriverequip.com/

Four Corners River Sports
360 S Camino Del Rio
Durango, CO 81302-0379
800-426-7637
http://www.riversports.com/

Gingerbrook Farm (maple syrup – the real deal)
621 White Hill Rd.
Washington, VT 05675
802-685-3061
jliddell@innevi.com

Nantahala Outdoor Center
13077 Hwy 19 West
Bryson City, NC 28713
800-367-3521
http://noc.com/

Northwest River Supplies
2009 S. Main St.
Moscow, ID 83843
800.635.5202
http://www.nrsweb.com/

Piragis Northwoods Company
105 N Central Avenue
Ely, MN 55731
800-223-6565
http://www.piragis.com/

Professional River Outfitters, Inc.
PO Box 635
Flagstaff, AZ 86002
800-648-3236
http://www.proriver.com/

REI
Sumner, WA 98352-0001
800-426-4840
http://www.rei.com/

River Connection
7121 SE Overland
Milwaukie, OR 97222
Phone: 503-788-3077
http://www.riverconnection.com/

RiverMaps
1540 S. Turnersville Rd.
Buda, TX 78610
512-295-2710
http://www.rivermaps.net/

Whole Earth Provision Company
2410 San Antonio St.
Austin, TX 78705-4815
512-478-1597
http://www.wholeearthprovision.com/

Recipe Index

This is an index of all the recipes in this book, with the page number of the menu where it appears. Menu items for which there are no recipes, such as crackers or wine, are not included.